WORLD IN *FLUX*

Time of Change

By

Eric Buffett

1

Table of Contents

Preface

The dawn of a new era, one marked by unparalleled opportunity and transformation, is upon us. Because of globalization, technological advancements, and a growing awareness of our interconnectedness, the world is changing quickly. Both the problems and the answers to them are intricate and multidimensional.

This book serves as an invitation to investigate the significant changes occurring in our world today. The opportunities and challenges that lie ahead are examined as it explores the major trends and forces influencing our future. We will examine the crucial topics that will shape the twenty-first century, from the emergence of artificial intelligence to the pressing effects of climate change.

In the ensuing pages, we will look at the following topics:

Technological Revolution: The effects of cutting-edge technologies like biotechnology, nanotechnology, and artificial intelligence will be examined.

Climate Change and Sustainability: The pressing need to tackle climate change and make the shift to a sustainable future will be covered.

We'll look at global inequality, including the widening wealth disparity and the obstacles to a more just society.

The evolving geopolitical environment and the emergence of new world powers will be examined.

The Future of Work: The effects of automation and artificial intelligence on the nature of work in the future will be examined.

This book is an invitation to consider the world we live in critically and to imagine a better future, not just a compilation of data. It is an appeal for people, groups, and governments to unite in order to tackle today's issues and create a more fair, sustainable, and just society.

It is important that we approach the future with optimism and hope as we set out on this journey. Making educated decisions and taking action that will benefit future generations is possible when we comprehend the forces influencing our world.

Part I:
The Shifting Landscape

Chapter 1:

A New Age Begins

The world is changing like never before. We are entering a new era of unprecedented technological advancement, global interconnectedness, and urgent environmental issues. In this new era, complex forces shape the future in their own ways.

The rapid acceleration of technological innovation drives change. AI, ML, and automation are changing industries, creating new opportunities, and disrupting work. Digital connectivity has enabled global collaboration and cultural exchange for billions. However, it has also raised concerns about privacy, security, and the potential for job displacement.

The interconnectedness of our world has never been more apparent. Global supply chains, international trade and the free flow of information have facilitated economic growth and cultural exchange. However, this interconnectedness has also made us more vulnerable to global crises, such as pandemics and economic downturns. The COVID-19 pandemic showed how fragile our globalized world is and the need for resilience and cooperation.

Earth and humanity face an existential threat from climate change. Rising global temperatures, extreme weather events, and environmental degradation are already having a profound impact on ecosystems and human societies. The need to transition to a sustainable future is urgent, requiring significant investments in renewable energy, clean technologies, and sustainable practices.

The geopolitical landscape is also undergoing significant shifts. The rise of new powers, the decline of traditional alliances, and the increasing competition for resources are reshaping the global balance of power. Geopolitical tensions and conflicts continue to pose a threat to peace and security while also creating opportunities for diplomacy and cooperation.

As we navigate this complex and uncertain landscape, it is essential to embrace change and adapt to the challenges and opportunities of the future. This requires a willingness to learn, innovate, and collaborate. It also requires a commitment to ethical principles, social justice, and environmental sustainability.

The new era offers both promise and peril. It is a time of great potential but also of great risk. By making informed choices and taking bold action, we can shape a future that is both prosperous and sustainable. We must work together to address the challenges of our time and build a better world for future generations.

Key themes of the new era:

Technological advancement: Rapid development of AI, machine learning, and automation.

Global interconnectedness: Increased globalization and interdependence.

Climate change: Urgent need for sustainable practices and renewable energy.

Geopolitical shifts: Changing power dynamics and emerging global players.

Social and economic inequality: Growing disparities and the need for equitable development.

Challenges and opportunities:

Job displacement: Automation and AI could lead to job losses.

Cybersecurity threats: Increased risk of cyberattacks and data breaches.

Climate change impacts: Rising sea levels, extreme weather events, and resource scarcity.

Geopolitical tensions: Potential for conflict and instability.

Social and economic inequality: Growing divide between the rich and poor.

Addressing the challenges and seizing the opportunities:

Invest in education and skills training. Prepare the workforce for the jobs of the future.

Promote innovation and entrepreneurship: Foster a culture of creativity and risk-taking.

Transition to a sustainable economy: Invest in renewable energy and sustainable practices.

Strengthen international cooperation: Address global challenges through multilateralism.

Promote social justice and equity: Reduce inequality and create opportunities for all.

By embracing the challenges and seizing the opportunities of this new era, we can build a better future for ourselves and for generations to come.

1.1 A Synopsis of Historical Eras of Major Transformation

Change, innovation, and upheaval are all woven into the fabric of human history. Societies have undergone periods of significant change over millennia, influencing the development of civilization. These eras, which saw profound changes in politics, economics, culture, and technology, have had a lasting impact on the world we live in today.

The Revolution in Agriculture

The Agricultural Revolution, which started about 10,000 years ago, was one of the most revolutionary eras in human history. Humans were hunter-gatherers before this, depending on hunting and foraging for food. This way of life was significantly altered by the domestication of plants and animals, which made it possible for agriculture and settled communities to flourish.

A surplus of food brought about by the Agricultural Revolution fueled population expansion and the rise of specialized labor. Societies' social structures, economic systems, and cultural customs all grew increasingly complex. This revolutionary time led to the creation of cities, writing systems, and organized religions.

The Revolution in Industry

Another turning point in human history was the Industrial Revolution, which started in Great Britain in the late 18th century. The development of steam-powered and later electrically powered machinery transformed communication, transportation, and manufacturing. Societies all over the world were altered by the Industrial Revolution's accompanying rapid urbanization and economic expansion.

Significant social and political changes were also brought about by the Industrial Revolution. This era had several effects, including the development of labor unions, the rise of the working class, and the call for social reforms. The Industrial Revolution shaped how we live, work, and relate to one another, laying the groundwork for the modern world.

The Age of Information

The quick development of information and communication technologies is what defines the Information Age, which started in the middle of the 20th century. The invention of the computer, the internet, and the smartphone has revolutionized the way we access, process, and share information.

The emergence of digital culture, the democratization of knowledge, and the globalization of economies are all results of the Information Age. Concerns regarding privacy, security, and the digital divide have also been brought up by it. Our world is still changing at breakneck speed due to technology, and its full impact is hard to foresee.

Other Times of Major Transformation

Throughout history, there have been many other times of substantial change in addition to these major ones. For instance, the Renaissance, a time of great artistic and cultural development in Europe, saw a resurgence of classical education and a shift toward humanism. The Enlightenment was an intellectual and philosophical movement that questioned established norms and supported individual liberty, reason, and science.

For decades, the world's political landscape was shaped by the Cold War, a time of geopolitical tension between the US and the USSR. A new era of globalization and economic interdependence began with the end of the Cold War.

Change's Future

Change will undoubtedly continue to be a constant as we look to the future. New technologies that have the potential to completely transform our lives include biotechnology, nanotechnology, and artificial intelligence. However, these technologies also raise ethical questions and pose challenges to society.

We must welcome change, adjust to new situations, and cooperate to create a better future in order to successfully negotiate the complexity of the twenty-first century. By learning from the past, we can anticipate the challenges and opportunities that lie ahead.

1.2 Finding the Distinctive Features of Our Present Time

The new era of the twenty-first century is characterized by a special fusion of societal changes, global interconnectedness, and technological breakthroughs. This era, which is sometimes called the Digital Age or the Information Age, differs from earlier historical eras in a number of important ways.

The Revolution in Digital

The quick development of digital technologies is one of the most distinctive features of our time. Artificial intelligence, smartphones, and the internet have completely changed how we work, communicate, and use information. The emergence of social media, e-commerce, and remote work as a result of the digital revolution has drastically changed how people interact with one another and conduct business.

Worldwide Interdependence

Thanks to developments in communication and transportation technologies, the world has grown more interconnected. A sense of global citizenship has been promoted, and conventional barriers have been dismantled by the globalization of economies, cultures, and ideas. We are now more susceptible to global issues like pandemics, climate change, and economic crises as a result of our interconnectedness.

Artificial Intelligence's Ascent

One significant force influencing our world is artificial intelligence (AI). Large-scale data analysis, task automation, and intelligent decision-making are all made possible by AI-powered systems. Although AI has enormous potential for creativity and problem-solving, it also brings up moral questions regarding privacy, job displacement, and abuse.

Environmental Challenges and Climate Change
Perhaps the most urgent issue of our day is climate change. The planet's ecosystems and human societies are in danger due to environmental degradation, extreme weather, and rising global temperatures. Making the shift to a sustainable future has gained international attention and calls for large investments in clean technologies, sustainable practices, and renewable energy.

The Economy of Knowledge

The nature of work has changed as a result of the transition from an industrial to a knowledge economy. Knowledge and innovation are the main forces behind economic growth in the modern world. As a result, there is an increasing need for highly qualified personnel, especially in disciplines like science, engineering, and technology.

Political and Social Transformation

Significant social and political change has occurred in the twenty-first century. The emergence of social movements like #MeToo and Black Lives Matter has raised awareness of gender and racial inequality. There is now more focus on cultural tolerance and understanding as a result of the growing diversity of societies. But in many regions of the world, social unrest and political polarization have also increased.

The Distinguishing Factors Between the Digital and Physical Worlds

Another aspect of our time that sets us apart is the merging of the digital and physical worlds. With billions of devices connected, the Internet of Things (IoT) has made data-driven insights, automation, and remote monitoring possible. Our perception of the world is changing as a result of virtual and augmented reality technologies, which make it harder to distinguish between the real and the virtual.

The Implications of Technology for Ethics

Numerous ethical concerns have been brought up by the speed at which technology is developing. Concerns about surveillance, privacy, and the moral application of AI are becoming more and more significant. The ethical ramifications of our technological decisions must be carefully considered as we negotiate the complexity of the twenty-first century.

There are a lot of opportunities and challenges in the twenty-first century. The future of humanity will be shaped by the distinctive features of this era, such as technological innovation, global interconnectedness, and environmental concerns. We can strive toward a more sustainable, just, and prosperous future by comprehending these trends and tackling the issues they present.

Chapter 2:

The Quickening Rate of Transformation

Technology breakthroughs, globalization, and societal changes are the main causes of the 21st century's unparalleled rate of change. At an incredible rate, industries, economies, and cultures are changing as a result of this acceleration of change.

Developments in Technology

The main force behind the quickening rate of change is technological innovation. The way we live, work, and interact is changing as a result of the quick development of digital technologies like artificial intelligence, machine learning, and the internet of things.

Artificial Intelligence (AI) is transforming a number of industries, including healthcare and finance. Large-scale data analysis, prediction, and automation are all made possible by

AI-powered systems, which boost productivity and creativity.

Machine Learning: A branch of artificial intelligence, machine learning allows computers to learn from data and gradually get better at what they do. Advanced robotics, personalized medicine, and self-driving cars are all being developed with this technology.

The Internet of Things (IoT) allows for data collection, remote monitoring, and automation by connecting billions of devices to the internet. Industries like manufacturing, agriculture, and healthcare are changing as a result of this technology.

Interconnectedness and Globalization

By linking people and economies worldwide, globalization has quickened the rate of change. More competition, innovation, and cross-cultural interaction have resulted from the unrestricted flow of capital, information, goods, and services. Globalization has, nevertheless, also exacerbated environmental problems, social unrest, and economic inequality.

Global Supply Chains: The production and distribution of goods and services on a worldwide scale is now feasible thanks to the intricate web of global supply chains. However, there may be serious economic repercussions if these supply chains are disrupted by events like pandemics or geopolitical conflicts.

Cultural Exchange: People from various cultures can now connect and exchange ideas thanks to the internet and social media. As a result, the world is now more connected and diverse.

Changes in Society

The rate of change is also accelerating due to societal changes like urbanization, demographic shifts, and shifting perspectives on work and family.

Demographic Shifts. Increasing migration, decreasing birth rates, and aging populations are changing economies and societies. The social security, healthcare, and educational systems are all impacted by these demographic changes.

Urbanization: As a result of cities' explosive growth, there is a growing need for infrastructure, housing, and transportation. Other issues brought on by urbanization include social inequality, traffic jams, and air pollution.

Shifting Perceptions of Work and Family: Conventional ideas of work and family are being challenged by the growth of the gig economy, remote work, and flexible work schedules. The workplace and how we manage work and personal life are changing as a result of these developments.

The Effects of Quickening Change

People, organizations, and societies are all being significantly impacted by the rapid pace of change.

Job Market Disruption: AI and automation are changing the labor market, displacing jobs and creating new ones.

Increasing Complexity: People must be resilient, adaptive, and lifelong learners due to the growing complexity of the global economy and society.

Ethical Challenges: As technology develops, ethical concerns regarding privacy, surveillance, and artificial intelligence are brought up.

Individuals and organizations must embrace innovation, adjust to new technologies, and hone their critical thinking and problem-solving abilities if they are to prosper in this age of rapid change. We can create a prosperous and sustainable future by comprehending the forces causing change and taking proactive measures to address the difficulties they present.

2.1 Technological advancements and their impact on society

For centuries, human progress has been fueled by technological advancements. The development of artificial intelligence and the invention of the wheel are just two examples of how technology has changed economies, societies, and cultures. Significant changes in how we live, work, and interact with one another have resulted from the rapid acceleration of technological innovation in recent decades.

The Revolution in Digital

With the advent of computers, the internet, and smartphones, the digital revolution has changed how we do business, communicate, and obtain information. Globally, the internet has brought billions of people together, removing barriers based on geography and promoting the exchange of ideas and cultures.

E-commerce: With a wide range of goods and services at customers' fingertips, online shopping has completely transformed the retail industry.

Social media: Websites like Facebook, Instagram, and Twitter have revolutionized social interaction by allowing people to communicate with friends and family around the world.

Remote Work: People can now work remotely from any location with an internet connection thanks to technological advancements.

Learning and Artificial Intelligence

Numerous industries could undergo a revolution thanks to machine learning and artificial intelligence (AI). Large-scale data analysis, prediction, and task automation are all made possible by AI-powered systems, which boost productivity and creativity.

Healthcare: AI is being used to diagnose illnesses, create new medications, and customize treatment regimens.

Finance: Algorithms driven by AI are used to identify fraud, evaluate risk, and offer tailored financial guidance.

Autonomous Vehicles: By lowering traffic and accident rates, self-driving cars have the potential to completely transform transportation.

Data collection, remote monitoring, and automation are made possible by the Internet of Things (IoT), which links billions of devices to the internet. Applications for IoT devices are numerous and include everything from industrial automation to smart homes.

Smart Homes: By automating functions like heating, lighting, and security, Internet of Things devices can improve the convenience and efficiency of homes.

Smart Cities: IoT technology is being applied to enhance public safety, lessen traffic, and optimize urban infrastructure.

The Effect on the Community

Both positive and negative effects of technological advancements on society have been significant.

Benefits:

Better Quality of Life: Technology has greatly enhanced communication, healthcare, and education, extending life expectancy and improving quality of life.

Economic Growth: By generating new markets, employment opportunities, and industries, technological innovation propels economic growth.

Global Connectivity: The internet has promoted international collaboration and dismantled barriers.

Adverse Effects:

Job displacement: In some industries, workers may be replaced by automation and artificial intelligence.

Privacy Issues: Data security and privacy are issues brought up by the growing use of technology.

Digital Divide: The wealth gap between the rich and the poor is caused by unequal access to technology.

It is crucial to create ethical standards, make training and education investments, and guarantee fair access to technology in order to lessen the negative effects of technological advancements. We can create a prosperous and sustainable future by embracing innovation and tackling the problems it presents.

2.2 The role of globalization in shaping our world

In recent decades, globalization—the growing interdependence of economies, cultures, and societies around the world—has changed the face of the planet. It has impacted cultural norms, changed geopolitical dynamics, and reshaped industries. The various ways that globalization has shaped our world will be examined in this essay.

Globalization of the Economy

National economies are now a part of the global economy as a result of economic globalization. The development of technology, the liberalization of capital flows, and the removal of trade barriers have all contributed to this integration. This facilitates the free flow of capital, goods, and services across international borders.

Advantages of Globalization in the Economy:

Increased economic growth: Trade and investment have increased as a result of globalization, which has boosted economic expansion and job creation.

Reduced costs for consumers: Globalization has contributed to lower costs for consumers by boosting competition.

Technological innovation: Innovation and technological breakthroughs have been facilitated by the cross-border exchange of ideas and knowledge.

Economic Globalization's Challenges:

Income inequality: Due to the relocation of jobs and wealth to areas with cheaper labor costs, globalization has made income inequality worse.

Employment displacement: In certain sectors and geographical areas, automation and outsourcing have resulted in job losses.

Impact on the environment: Growing production and consumption have exacerbated climate change and environmental deterioration.

Globalization of Culture

The term *"cultural globalization"* describes the cross-border dissemination of cultural goods and concepts. Migration, international travel, and the expansion of mass media have all made this easier.

Cultural globalization's advantages

Cultural exchange: As a result of globalization, people now understand and value other cultures more.

Enhanced diversity: A more multicultural and varied world has resulted from the blending of cultures.

Dismantling cultural barriers: Globalization has aided in the dismantling of cultural barriers and the advancement of tolerance and comprehension.

Cultural Globalization's Challenges:

Cultural homogenization: Local customs and cultures may be lost as a result of Western culture's hegemony.
Cultural imperialism: This refers to the practice of forcing Western norms and values on non-Western cultures.

Globalization of Politics

The term *"political globalization"* describes how political systems are becoming more interconnected and international organizations are becoming more influential. As a result, international organizations now hold more power than nation-states.

Political globalization's advantages

International cooperation: On topics like human rights, terrorism, and climate change, globalization has made it easier for nations to work together.

Promotion of human rights and democracy: International organizations have contributed to the advancement of these two concepts.

Political Globalization's Challenges:

Loss of national sovereignty: Nation-states' sovereignty may be undermined by the growing power of international organizations.
Challenges in global governance: Addressing global issues may become difficult if there is ineffective global governance.

Globalization's Future

Since growing nationalism, protectionism, and geopolitical tensions may impede further integration, the future of globalization is uncertain. Globalization will probably continue to be fueled by technological developments and the growing interdependence of the world economy, nevertheless.

Adopting policies that support fair growth, safeguard the environment, and respect human rights is crucial to minimizing the negative effects of globalization and maximizing its positive effects. Together, nations can create a more equitable, sustainable, and prosperous future for everybody.

2.3 The Development of Political and Social Movements

A wide range of issues, from social justice and climate change to economic inequality and political corruption, have fueled a resurgence of social and political movements in the twenty-first century. To question the status quo and call for change, these movements have employed a range of strategies, such as boycotts, strikes, protests, and online activism.

Important Forces Behind Political and Social Movements

In recent years, social and political movements have grown in popularity due to a number of factors:

Social Media and Digital Activism: People can now connect, organize, and mobilize globally thanks to social media platforms. These platforms have made it easier for information to spread quickly, which has helped movements gain traction and garner a lot of attention.

Economic Inequality: Social unrest and discontent have been exacerbated by growing economic inequality. People are calling for more equitable wealth distribution and economic justice as the gap between the rich and the poor grows.

Climate Change: Millions of people are calling on governments and businesses to take action in response to the pressing threat posed by climate change. Ambitious climate policies, renewable energy, and sustainable practices have all been demanded by climate change movements.

Social Justice Issues: Concerns like LGBTQ+ rights, gender inequality, and racial injustice have spurred a lot of activism and protests. These topics are now at the forefront of public conversation thanks to movements like #MeToo and Black Lives Matter.

Political Polarization: Populist movements have grown in popularity, and traditional institutions are losing credibility as a result of the growing polarization of political discourse. New social and political movements have been able to flourish as a result.

Social and political movements' effects

Public opinion, policy decisions, and social change have all been significantly impacted by social and political movements.

Public Awareness: By mobilizing public opinion and applying pressure to decision-makers, movements have brought attention to urgent social and political issues.

Significant policy changes have resulted from successful movements, such as the anti-apartheid movement in South Africa and the civil rights movement in the United States.

Social Change: Social tolerance, equality, and justice have grown as a result of movements that have questioned conventional wisdom.

Empowerment of Marginalized Groups: Movements have given marginalized groups the ability to engage in politics and demand their rights.

Opportunities and Difficulties

Political and social movements can bring about constructive change, but they also face many obstacles:

Maintaining Momentum: It can be challenging to keep up momentum over time, particularly when faced with obstacles and setbacks.

Internal Conflicts: Internal conflict and divisions can undermine the effectiveness of movements.

Government Repression: To quell dissent and thwart the initiatives of social movements, governments may employ repressive measures. Social and political movements continue to be a potent force for change in spite of these obstacles. These movements can continue to influence our society's future by utilizing technology, forming alliances, and staying focused on long-term objectives.

Recognizing the contribution of social and political movements to solving the urgent issues of our day is crucial as we go forward. These movements have the potential to contribute to the creation of a more sustainable, just, and equitable world by empowering both individuals and communities.

Chapter 3:

Climate Change and Its Consequences

A worldwide phenomenon caused by human activity, climate change is one of the most urgent issues of our day. Global temperatures have significantly increased as a result of the excessive release of greenhouse gases, mainly carbon dioxide, into the atmosphere. This has had far-reaching effects on the planet and its people.

The Science of Climate Change

Ocean currents, greenhouse gases, and solar radiation are just a few of the many variables that interact intricately to form the Earth's climate system. The earth warms as a result of greenhouse gases like carbon dioxide, methane, and nitrous oxide trapping heat in the atmosphere. A warming trend has resulted from human activities, especially the burning of fossil fuels for energy, which has greatly raised the concentration of greenhouse gases in the atmosphere.

The Effects of Global Warming

Global ecosystems, economies, and societies are all impacted by the extensive and complex effects of climate change.

Among the most noteworthy effects are:

Increasing Global Temperatures: Heatwaves, droughts, and wildfires have become more frequent and intense as a result of the average global temperature's steady rise.

Extreme Weather Events: Hurricanes, floods, and droughts are among the extreme weather events that climate change is making worse. These occurrences have the potential to seriously harm human settlements, agriculture, and infrastructure.

Sea-Level Rise: Glaciers and ice sheets are melting as a result of rising global temperatures, which raises sea levels. Small island nations and coastal cities are seriously threatened by this.

Ocean Acidification: The absorption of excess carbon dioxide by the oceans is leading to ocean acidification, which threatens marine ecosystems and biodiversity.

Disruption of Ecosystems: Climate change is disrupting ecosystems, leading to the loss of biodiversity and the decline of species.

Impact on Human Health: Climate change can lead to increased heat-related illnesses, the spread of diseases, and mental health problems.

Reducing the Impact of Climate Change

To mitigate the effects of climate change, it is imperative to reduce greenhouse gas emissions and transition to a low-carbon economy.

A number of tactics can be used to accomplish this:

Renewable Energy: Shifting to renewable energy sources, such as solar, wind, and hydro power, can significantly reduce greenhouse gas emissions.

Energy Efficiency: Improving energy efficiency in buildings, transportation, and industry can help reduce energy consumption and emissions.

Carbon Capture and Storage: Carbon capture and storage technologies can capture and store carbon dioxide emissions from power plants and industrial facilities.

Sustainable Agriculture: Sustainable agricultural practices, such as agroforestry and organic farming, can reduce greenhouse gas emissions and improve soil health.

Afforestation and Reforestation: Planting trees can help absorb carbon dioxide from the atmosphere and restore degraded forests.

International Cooperation: International cooperation is essential to address climate change, as it requires a global effort to reduce emissions and adapt to the impacts of climate change.

Climate Change Adaptation

While mitigating climate change is crucial, it is equally important to adapt to its impacts. Adaptation strategies can help reduce the vulnerability of societies to climate change and build resilience.

Some key adaptation strategies include:

Infrastructure Development: Building resilient infrastructure, such as flood defenses and heat-resistant buildings, can help protect communities from climate-related disasters.

Water Management: Efficient water management practices, such as rainwater harvesting and water conservation, can help address water scarcity.

Early Warning Systems: Early warning systems can help communities prepare for and respond to extreme weather events.

Climate-Smart Agriculture: Adopting climate-smart agricultural practices can help farmers adapt to changing climatic conditions and ensure food security.

Disaster Risk Reduction: Investing in disaster risk reduction measures, such as disaster preparedness and response plans, can help minimize the impact of climate-related disasters.

By understanding the science behind climate change, the consequences it poses, and the strategies to mitigate and adapt to it, we can work towards a more sustainable future. International cooperation, technological innovation, and individual actions are all essential to addressing this global challenge.

3.1 The science behind climate change

The growing amount of greenhouse gases in the Earth's atmosphere is the primary cause of the complicated phenomenon known as climate change. The planet warms as a result of these gases' ability to retain solar heat. Although there have been natural climate fluctuations throughout Earth's history, human activity is largely to blame for the current, sharp warming trend.

The Effect of Greenhouses

The Earth's surface remains warm due to a natural process called the greenhouse effect. After being absorbed at the Earth's surface, sunlight is reemitted as infrared radiation. This infrared radiation is trapped by greenhouse gases in the atmosphere, including carbon dioxide, methane, and nitrous oxide, which stop it from escaping into space. The earth warms as a result of this trapped heat.

Human Activity and Emissions of Greenhouse Gases

The amount of greenhouse gases in the atmosphere has dramatically increased as a result of human activity, especially the burning of fossil fuels like coal, oil, and natural gas.

Greenhouse gas emissions are also caused by other human activities like industrial agriculture and deforestation.

Carbon Dioxide (CO2): Burning fossil fuels, deforestation, and industrial processes all contribute to the atmospheric release of CO2, the main greenhouse gas.

CH4 (methane): The production of fossil fuels, waste decomposition, and agriculture are some of the sources of methane, a powerful greenhouse gas.

Nitrous Oxide (N2O): The burning of fossil fuels, industrial operations, and agricultural practices all release nitrous oxide.

The Climate Change Evidence

The overwhelming body of evidence supporting climate change comes from several sources:

Temperature Records: Over the past century, there has been a noticeable warming trend in global temperature records.

practices and constructing resilient infrastructure.

3.2 The impact of climate change on ecosystems and human societies

Globally, ecosystems and human societies are being significantly impacted by climate change, which is being caused by the rising concentration of greenhouse gases in the atmosphere. The effects on human and natural systems are profound as sea levels rise, extreme weather events increase in frequency and severity, and global temperatures rise.

Ecosystem Impact

Globally, ecosystems are being upset by climate change, which is causing biodiversity loss, changes to food webs, and ecosystem collapse.

Among the main effects are:

Temperature Rise: The behavior, distribution, and phenology of plants and animals can all be altered by rising temperatures. Numerous species might find it difficult to adjust to these quick changes, which could result in population decreases and extinction.

Ocean Acidification: The oceans' absorption of too much carbon dioxide is causing the oceans to become more acidic, endangering marine ecosystems, especially coral reefs and shellfish.

Extreme Weather Events: Droughts, floods, and wildfires are examples of extreme weather events that can destroy ecosystems, resulting in habitat loss, a decline in species, and soil erosion.

Modified Precipitation Patterns: Ecosystems and human societies are both impacted by altered precipitation patterns, which can cause flooding in some areas and water scarcity in others.

Effects on Human Communities

Human societies are also being significantly impacted by climate change, which has an effect on economic activity, human health, water resources, and food security.

Among the main effects are:

Food Security: Food shortages and price increases may result from climate change's disruption of agricultural production. Food insecurity can be made worse by extreme weather events like droughts and floods, which can harm livestock and crops.

Water Scarcity: Many areas may experience water scarcity as a result of altered precipitation patterns brought on by climate change. Water use in homes, businesses, and agriculture may be impacted by this.

Human Health: The spread of diseases, an increase in heat-related illnesses, and mental health issues are all consequences of climate change. Injury and fatalities can also result from extreme weather events.

Economic Effects: A number of industries, including agriculture, tourism, and insurance, may be significantly impacted by climate change. Small island nations and coastal cities are especially susceptible to the negative economic effects of extreme weather events and sea level rise.

Migration and Displacement: As a result of droughts, rising sea levels, and other climate-related disasters, people may be compelled to relocate, which can result in migration and displacement.

Climate Change Adaptation

Governments and individuals alike must act to cut greenhouse gas emissions and prepare for climate change in order to lessen its effects.

Among the crucial tactics are:

Reducing Greenhouse Gas Emissions: Greenhouse gas emissions can be decreased by switching to renewable energy sources, increasing energy efficiency, and implementing sustainable practices.

Climate-Smart Agriculture: Farmers can improve agricultural productivity and adapt to climate change by putting climate-smart agricultural techniques like agroforestry and conservation agriculture into practice.

Water Resource Management: Water scarcity can be addressed with effective water management techniques like rainwater collection and water conservation.

Infrastructure Development: Communities can be shielded from climate-related disasters by investing in resilient infrastructure, such as flood defenses and heat-resistant structures.

Early Warning Systems: Communities can better prepare for and handle extreme weather events with the aid of early warning systems.

International Cooperation: Since reducing emissions and adapting to the effects of climate change necessitate a global effort, international cooperation is crucial.

We can strive toward a more sustainable future for people and the environment by acting now to cut greenhouse gas emissions and prepare for the effects of climate change.

3.3 Mitigation and adaptation strategies

Our planet and its people are seriously threatened by climate change. A mix of adaptation and mitigation techniques is required to meet this challenge. While adaptation strategies concentrate on lessening the adverse effects of climate change, mitigation strategies seek to lower greenhouse gas emissions.

Strategies for Mitigation

Reducing greenhouse gas emissions and shifting to a low-carbon economy are two mitigation strategies.

Important mitigation techniques consist of:

Sustainable Energy:

Solar energy is the process of using solar panels to capture solar radiation.

Wind Energy: Using wind turbines to transform wind energy into electrical power.
Using the kinetic energy of flowing water to generate electricity is known as hydropower.
Geothermal energy is the process of producing electricity by harnessing the heat that exists within the Earth.
Making energy from biomass, such as wood and agricultural waste, is known as bioenergy.

Efficiency of Energy:

Greenhouse gas emissions can be considerably decreased by increasing the energy efficiency of industry, transportation, and buildings.
Better insulation, LED lighting, and energy-efficient appliances can all contribute to lower energy usage.

Reliance on vehicles that run on fossil fuels can be decreased by encouraging walking, bicycling, and public transit.

Capturing and Storing Carbon (CCS):

Capturing and storing carbon dioxide emissions from factories and power plants underground. Although CCS is a sophisticated and costly technology, it can aid in lowering emissions from major point sources.

Tree Planting and Tree Reforestation:

Restoring degraded forests and removing carbon dioxide from the atmosphere are two benefits of planting trees.
Forests are essential for controlling the climate and supplying habitat for various species.

Agriculture that is sustainable:

Greenhouse gas emissions from agriculture can be decreased by implementing sustainable farming methods like agroforestry and conservation tillage.

Reducing the use of chemical pesticides and fertilizers, conserving water, and enhancing soil health are all benefits of sustainable agriculture.

International Collaboration:

Since reducing emissions and adapting to the effects of climate change necessitate a global effort, international cooperation is crucial.

A historic international pact known as the Paris Agreement seeks to keep global warming well below 2 degrees Celsius.

Strategies for Adaptation

The main goals of adaptation strategies are to lessen the adverse effects of climate change and increase resistance to risks associated with it.

Important adaptation techniques consist of:

Development of Infrastructure:

Communities can be protected from climate-related disasters by constructing resilient infrastructure, such as sea walls, flood defenses, and heat-resistant structures.
Building resilience to climate change and lowering greenhouse gas emissions are two benefits of investing in sustainable infrastructure.

Management of Water Resources:

Water scarcity can be addressed by putting effective water management techniques into place, such as rainwater collection and water conservation.
Water security can be ensured by making investments in water infrastructure, such as reservoirs and dams.

Climate-Aware Farming:

Farmers can improve agricultural productivity and adapt to climate change by implementing climate-smart farming techniques like agroforestry and conservation agriculture.
Farmers can also adapt to changing climate conditions by increasing irrigation systems, using drought-resistant seeds, and diversifying their crop production.

Systems for Early Warning:

Communities can better prepare for and handle extreme weather events like hurricanes, floods, and heat waves with the aid of early warning systems.
By giving people timely notice of approaching disasters, these systems enable them to take precautions and evacuate.

Ecological-Based Adjustment:

Resilience to climate change can be increased by preserving and repairing ecosystems.
Numerous advantages, including flood protection, biodiversity preservation, and carbon sequestration, can be obtained from healthy ecosystems.

Adaptation Based on the Community:

Involving communities in the creation and application of adaptation plans can guarantee that their priorities and needs are met.
Additionally, communities can be empowered to take charge of their own resilience through community-based adaptation.
We can limit the negative effects of climate change and work toward a more sustainable future by combining adaptation and mitigation strategies. To solve this global issue and secure the welfare of future generations, urgent action is required.

Part II:
Navigating Uncertainty

Chapter 4:

Economic Disruption and Inequality:

Globalization, changing geopolitical dynamics, and technological advancements are all contributing to the current period of profound disruption in the global economy. Economic inequality is rising as a result of these shifts in labor markets, industries, and income distribution.

Disruption by Technology

Automation, robotics, artificial intelligence, and other technological developments are changing labor markets and industries. These technologies have the potential to boost creativity and productivity, but they also put jobs and livelihoods at risk. Workers may be displaced or compelled to learn new skills as machines become more proficient at tasks that have historically been performed by humans.

Effect on Employment:

Job Displacement: In sectors like manufacturing, transportation, and customer service, automation and artificial intelligence may result in job losses.

Employment Creation: New technologies have the potential to generate employment, especially in fields like renewable energy, healthcare, and technology.

Skill Mismatch: Because technology is changing so quickly, there may be a discrepancy between the skills that employers need and those that employees already possess.

World War II

National economies have become more integrated as a result of globalization, which has made it easier for capital, labor, goods, and services to move across national boundaries. Although many have benefited from globalization, economic inequality has also increased as a result of it.

Effect on Inequality:

Wage Inequality: As businesses look to cut costs by outsourcing production to lower-wage nations, global competition may cause wages in developed nations to decline.

Income Inequality: Income inequality may be made worse by the concentration of wealth in the hands of a small number of people and businesses.

Changes in Geopolitics

Global supply chains can be disrupted and economic uncertainty raised by geopolitical changes like trade wars and tensions. Price increases, slower economic growth, and job losses are all possible outcomes of these disruptions.

Effect on the Economy:

Trade Wars: Trade wars have the potential to raise trade barriers and tariffs, which would raise the price of goods and services.
Natural disasters and geopolitical unrest can cause supply chain disruptions that result in shortages and price increases worldwide.
Economic Uncertainty: Political unpredictability and instability have the potential to deter investment and impede economic expansion.

Resolving Inequality and Economic Disruption

A variety of laws and tactics can be used to lessen the detrimental effects of inequality and economic disruption.

Education and Training: Funding education and training initiatives can assist employees in gaining the competencies required to thrive in the economy of the twenty-first century.
Social Safety Nets: During times of economic upheaval, workers can be protected by robust

social safety nets, such as social welfare programs and unemployment insurance.

Progressive Taxation: By taxing higher earners at a higher rate, progressive taxation can aid in the reduction of income inequality.

Labor Market Regulations: Strict labor market laws can guarantee fair compensation and safeguard employees' rights.

International Cooperation: To address issues like trade imbalances, tax evasion, and climate change, international cooperation is crucial.

The underlying causes of inequality and economic disruption can be addressed by policymakers to build a more sustainable and equitable future for everybody.

4.1 The changing nature of work

Globalization, changing societal values, and technological advancements are all contributing to a significant transformation in the nature of work. The way we work, job markets, and industries are all changing as a result of these developments.

The Development of Technology

The workplace has been completely transformed by technological innovations like automation, artificial intelligence, and the internet. Technology is changing industries, generating new employment opportunities, and dislodging traditional roles as it develops further.

Automation: Routine and repetitive tasks are increasingly being replaced by automation, which is displacing workers in customer service, logistics, and manufacturing.
Artificial Intelligence: Systems with AI capabilities can carry out difficult tasks like data analysis, judgment, and original problem-solving. Numerous sectors, including healthcare and finance, could be affected by this.

Remote Work: Employees can now work from any location with an internet connection thanks to the growing popularity of remote work, which makes it harder to distinguish between work and personal life.

The gig economy

In recent years, the gig economy—which is defined by temporary, flexible work arrangements—has expanded dramatically. Freelancers, independent contractors, and platform workers are examples of gig workers who can work on several projects at once and have more control over their work schedules.

Flexibility, independence, and the chance to work on a variety of projects are advantages of the gig economy.
The gig economy's challenges include: unstable income, few benefits, and a lack of job security.

Work's Future

Automation, greater flexibility, and the emergence of new job roles are likely to define the nature of work in the future.

Among the new trends are:

Remote Work: As technology makes it possible for more people to work from anywhere, remote work is predicted to continue to gain traction.
Freelancing and Gig Work: As the gig economy grows, workers will have more flexibility, but they will also need to be more flexible and enterprising.
AI and Automation: These two technologies will keep changing industries, displacing existing jobs and generating new ones.
The Knowledge Worker's Ascent: There will be a greater need for highly skilled workers as the economy moves toward knowledge-based industries.
Soft skills like creativity, critical thinking, and emotional intelligence will become even more

important in a world that is becoming more and more automated.

Adjusting to the Changing Work Environment

In order to prosper in the evolving workplace, people and organizations need to be open to embracing new technologies and methods of operation.

The following are some tactics for adjusting to the evolving nature of work:

Lifelong Learning: To remain competitive in the labor market, one must constantly learn new things and develop new abilities.

Developing Soft Skills: In the contemporary workplace, having strong interpersonal, communication, and problem-solving abilities is essential for success.

Embracing Technology: Being able to use new tools and technologies can make people and organizations more productive and efficient.

Creating Powerful Networks: Connecting with other professionals can help people work together on projects and discover new employment opportunities.

Developing Entrepreneurial Skills: In the gig economy and when launching a business, entrepreneurial abilities like creativity, innovation, and risk-taking can be beneficial.

Although the future of work is uncertain, people and organizations can successfully navigate the opportunities and challenges of the workplace in the twenty-first century by embracing change and making investments in education and skills.

4.2 The rise of automation and artificial intelligence

Globally, industries, economies, and societies are changing as a result of the quick development of automation and artificial intelligence (AI). The way we live, work, and engage with the world is changing as a result of these technologies.

Automation: Increasing Efficiency by Automating Tasks

Automation is the use of technology to carry out tasks that were previously completed by people. Simple jobs like putting things together on a production line or more complicated jobs like operating a vehicle or doing data analysis can fall under this category.

Advantages of Automation

Enhanced Productivity and Efficiency: By decreasing human error and expediting procedures, automation can greatly boost productivity and efficiency.

Decreased Costs: Businesses can increase their profitability and cut labor expenses by automating tasks.

Better Quality: By lowering variability and guaranteeing consistency, automation can contribute to better quality goods and services.

Automation's drawbacks

Job displacement: Automation has the potential to eliminate jobs, especially in sectors of the economy that mainly depend on manual labor.

Skill Mismatch: As automation develops, workers might need to pick up new abilities to stay in demand.

Ethical Issues: The application of automation presents ethical issues, including the possibility of prejudice and discrimination.

Intelligent Machines: Artificial Intelligence

The creation of computer systems that are capable of learning, reasoning, and problem-solving—tasks that normally require human intelligence—is referred to as artificial intelligence. AI has the potential to completely transform a wide range of sectors, including finance and healthcare.

AI types include:

Narrow AI refers to AI programs created to carry out particular functions, like language translation or facial recognition.
General AI refers to AI systems that are intelligent enough to comprehend and learn any intellectual task at the level of a human.

AI's effects:

Healthcare: AI can be used to create new medications, analyze medical images, and customize treatment regimens.
Finance: AI can be used to evaluate risk, identify fraud, and offer tailored financial advice.
Transportation: Self-driving cars with AI capabilities have the potential to completely transform transportation by lowering accident rates and enhancing traffic flow.

Customer service: AI-driven chatbots are able to offer round-the-clock assistance by responding to inquiries and fixing problems.

The Future of Work Automation and artificial intelligence are changing the nature of work. These technologies present difficulties for the labor market even though they have the potential to increase productivity and generate new jobs.

In order to adjust to the evolving nature of work, people and organizations need to:

Lifelong Learning: To remain competitive in the labor market, one must constantly learn new things and develop new abilities.

Reskilling and Upskilling: In order to adjust to the shifting demands of the workplace, employees may need to reskill or upskill.

Human-Machine Collaboration: Humans and machines can cooperate to produce better results.

Ethical Considerations: It is imperative to take into account the ethical ramifications automation and artificial intelligence, including issues of bias, privacy, and job displacement.

Although the future of work is uncertain, we can use automation and artificial intelligence (AI) to build a more prosperous and just future by embracing technological advancements and adjusting to the shifting landscape.

4.3 Social Unrest and Income Inequality

Throughout history, income inequality—the unequal distribution of wealth and income within a society—has been a recurring problem. Nonetheless, in many nations, the wealth disparity has grown dramatically in recent decades. A number of social and political issues, such as political instability, social unrest, and a loss of social cohesiveness, have been connected to this rising inequality.

The Reasons Behind Inequality in Income

The rise in income inequality has been attributed to a number of factors:

Technological Developments: Automation and artificial intelligence are two examples of technological developments that have resulted in job displacement and a rise in demand for highly skilled workers. Because high-skilled workers command higher wages and low-skilled workers find it difficult to find employment, this has made income inequality worse.

Globalization: Jobs have become more competitive as a result of globalization, especially in low-skilled service and manufacturing sectors. Many workers' wages have been under pressure to decline as a result. Income inequality may be exacerbated by tax policies, such as reduced tax rates for corporations and high-income individuals.

Labor Union Decline: Workers' bargaining power has been undermined by the decline of labor unions, which has resulted in lower wages and fewer benefits.

The economy has become more financialized as a result of speculation and finance's growing power, which has concentrated wealth in a small number of hands.

The Effects of Inequality on Society and Politics

There may be serious social and political repercussions from income inequality.

Social Unrest: When people are angry about the unequal distribution of opportunities and wealth, high levels of inequality can cause social unrest. Riots, protests, and other types of civil disobedience can be examples of this.

Political Instability: By fostering political polarization, populism, and extremism, inequality can threaten political stability. Additionally, it may result incrony capitalism and corruption.

Weakening of Social Cohesion: By dividing various socioeconomic groups, inequality can weaken social cohesion. Increased crime, violence, and social unrest may result from this.

Health and Well-Being: Since those from lower socioeconomic backgrounds are more likely to suffer from poor health outcomes, inequality can have a detrimental effect on health and well-being.

Decreased Economic Growth: By lowering consumer demand, restricting investment, and escalating social and political instability, inequality can impede economic growth.

Resolving Income Inequality

A variety of laws and tactics can be put into place to combat income disparity and its detrimental effects.

Progressive Taxation: By taxing high-income earners more heavily, progressive taxation can aid in the reduction of income inequality.

Increasing Labor Union Strength: Increasing labor union strength can help raise workers' wages and bargaining power.

Putting Money Into Education and Training: Putting money into education and training can help give employees the tools they need to thrive in the economy of the twenty-first century.

Social Safety Nets: Vulnerable populations can be protected by robust social safety nets, such as social welfare programs and unemployment insurance.

Lowering Obstacles to Entrepreneurship: Lowering obstacles to entrepreneurship can support economic expansion and the creation of new jobs.

International Cooperation: Addressing global economic inequality and advancing fair trade practices require international cooperation.

Governments and societies can strive toward a more just and equitable future by tackling the underlying causes of income inequality and putting in place efficient policies.

Chapter 5 :

Conflict and Geopolitical Tensions

Throughout human history, geopolitical tensions and conflicts have persisted. Territorial conflicts, ideological disagreements, economic rivalry, and cultural conflicts are some of the causes of these tensions. With the emergence of new powers, the dissolution of long-standing alliances, and the growing interdependence of the global economy, the world landscape has grown more complicated in recent years.

Principal Causes of Geopolitical Conflicts

Geopolitical tensions and conflict are caused by a number of factors:

Great Power Competition: Strategic rivalry and geopolitical tensions have escalated as a result of the resurgence of great power competition, especially between the US and China. This competition is taking place in a number of areas, such as trade, technology, and military might.

Regional Conflicts: The world order is still unstable due to regional conflicts like those in the Middle East and Africa. Ethnic and sectarian divisions, territorial disputes, and the competition for resources are frequently the causes of these conflicts.

Risks to Cybersecurity: Cyberattacks have become a serious danger to critical infrastructure, economic stability, and national security. Governments, corporations, and individuals are constantly at risk from state-sponsored hacking organizations and cybercriminals.

Climate Change: By creating mass migration and displacement and intensifying competition for resources like food and water, climate change is escalating geopolitical tensions.

Nuclear Proliferation: A major danger to international security is the spread of nuclear weapons. There is still a serious risk of war, terrorism, and nuclear accidents.

Geopolitical Tensions' Effects

Human rights, security, and the world economy are all significantly impacted by geopolitical tensions and conflicts.

Among the main repercussions are:

Economic Disruption: Trade barriers, global supply chains, and economic uncertainty can all be caused by geopolitical tensions.

Military Conflict: In severe circumstances, geopolitical tensions may turn into a war, which would result in fatalities, infrastructure damage, and population displacement.

Humanitarian Crises: Famine, illness, and mass displacement are examples of humanitarian crises that can result from conflicts.

Cyberattacks: Cyberattacks have the potential to destroy economies, steal private data, and interfere with vital infrastructure.

Nuclear Proliferation: The spread of nuclear weapons raises the possibility of a nuclear conflict, which might have disastrous effects on humanity.

Reducing Geopolitical Conflicts

In order to reduce geopolitical tensions and avert war, it is crucial to:

One of the most important strategies for settling disagreements and averting conflict is diplomacy. Building trust and understanding between countries can be facilitated by diplomatic communication and negotiation.

International Cooperation: To address global issues like terrorism, nuclear proliferation, and climate change, international cooperation is crucial.

Arms Control: Agreements pertaining to arms control can lessen the likelihood of nuclear proliferation and armed conflict.

Economic Integration: By encouraging trade, investment, and collaboration, economic integration can aid in the reduction of tensions.

Cultural Exchange: Cultural exchange can foster understanding and help to create bridges between various cultures.

Nations can lessen geopolitical tensions and build a more prosperous and peaceful world by cooperating. But there are a lot of obstacles to overcome, and achieving these objectives will take perseverance and dedication.

5.1 The decline of traditional power structures

Traditional power structures have significantly weakened in the twenty-first century, as evidenced by the emergence of new non-state actors and the deterioration of nation-state authority. Numerous factors, such as globalization, technological advancements, and shifting societal values, are responsible for this shift.

National Sovereignty's Decline

Globalization and the emergence of transnational actors are posing a growing threat to the idea of national sovereignty, which was once a fundamental component of the international system. Nation-states are losing some of their historical power as economies grow more interconnected and information travels more freely across national boundaries.

Globalization: Nation-states' authority over their economies and societies has been undermined by the globalization of trade, finance, and culture. For instance, multinational firms frequently conduct business internationally and have a big impact on national economies.

Technological Developments: The internet and social media, among other technological developments, have given people and organizations the ability to question governmental power. Information dissemination, social movement mobilization, and cross-border activity coordination have all been made easier by these technologies.

Rise of Non-State Actors: Non-state actors, including transnational corporations, international organizations, and NGOs, have become more and more influential in world affairs. These players have the power to influence governments, mobilize public opinion, and set policy agendas.

New Power Centers' Ascent

New power centers are appearing as established power structures deteriorate. These new hubs could be founded on cultural, technological, or economic dominance.

Economic Power: Traditional powers' hegemony is coming under increasing pressure from nations with robust economies, like China and

India. Through trade, investment, and financial clout, these nations can influence the world economy.

Power in Technology: Nations with advanced technology, like China and the United States, are at the forefront of technological advancement, which can have important geopolitical ramifications.

Cultural Power: Nations with significant cultural sway, like South Korea and the United States, have the ability to influence international trends in music, fashion, and film.

The Consequences of Rejecting Power Systems

There are several ramifications for international politics and security from the breakdown of established power structures:

Increasing Complexity: With numerous players fighting for sway, the world political scene is getting more complicated. Increased rivalry, conflict, and uncertainty may result from this.

Rise of Nationalism and Populism: As people look to reclaim their identity and sovereignty, the breakdown of established power structures can feed nationalism and populism.

Global Governance Challenges: Addressing global issues like poverty, terrorism, and climate change may become more challenging as nation-states become less powerful.

Enhanced Security Risks: The growth of non-state actors, including cybercriminals and terrorist organizations, can be a serious danger to international security.

One important trend that is changing the political landscape globally is the breakdown of traditional power structures. To meet the opportunities and challenges of the twenty-first century, new approaches to cooperation and governance must be developed as the world grows more interconnected and complex.

5.2 The rise of nationalism and populism

Nationalism and populism have been on the rise all over the world in recent years. Numerous factors, such as political polarization, cultural anxieties, and economic inequality, have contributed to this trend.

What Nationalism and Populism Are

Nationalism: This ideology places a strong emphasis on allegiance, devotion, and loyalty to a country or nation-state. Nationalists frequently put their country's interests ahead of those of other countries.

A political philosophy known as populism sets a morally upright populace against a dishonest ruling class. Populist leaders frequently appeal to people's emotions and offer straightforward answers to difficult issues.

Factors Contributing to the Growth of Populism and Nationalism

Economic Inequality: Many people, especially those who have been left behind by globalization, have experienced feelings of resentment and frustration as a result of economic inequality. By vowing to uphold the rights of the working class and take harsh measures against the wealthy elite, populist leaders frequently take advantage of these sentiments.

Cultural Anxiety: Nationalist and populist movements have gained traction due to cultural concerns about immigration, globalization, and the decline of traditional values. These movements frequently demonize foreigners and immigrants while advancing a limited and exclusive definition of national identity.

Political Polarization: Politicians have found it challenging to reach a compromise and find common ground as a result of political polarization. This has given populist leaders the chance to take advantage of social divisions and rally support.

Decline of Traditional Media: Misinformation and disinformation have been able to proliferate more readily as a result of the traditional media's decline. Social media and other online channels are frequently used by populist leaders to mobilize their followers and disseminate their message.

The Effects of Populism and Nationalism

International relations and world politics have been significantly impacted by the rise of nationalism and populism.

Among the main repercussions are:

Increasing Political Polarization: To rally their followers and disparage their rivals, nationalist and populist leaders frequently employ divisive rhetoric. Social unrest and heightened political polarization may result from this.

Erosion of Democratic Norms: Populist leaders have the potential to erode democratic norms and institutions, including the rule of law, freedom of the press, and freedom of speech.

Isolationism and Protectionism: Populist and nationalist leaders frequently advocate isolationist foreign and trade policies. International cooperation and economic growth may suffer as a result.

Enhanced International Tensions: Aggressive foreign policies by nationalist and populist leaders may exacerbate tensions between nations.

Weakening of International Institutions: The legitimacy of international organizations like the European Union and the United Nations may be questioned by nationalist and populist leaders.

Taking on the Problems of Populism and Nationalism

Addressing the issues raised by populism and nationalism requires:

Encourage Tolerance and Diversity: Nationalist and populist leaders' polarizing rhetoric can be repelled by promoting tolerance and diversity.

Strengthen Democratic Institutions: One way to guard against the deterioration of democratic norms is to strengthen democratic institutions like the legislature and the judiciary.

Fight Misinformation and Disinformation: One way to stop the spread of misinformation and disinformation is to encourage media literacy and critical thinking.

Tackling Economic Inequality: Populist and nationalist movements may become less appealing if economic inequality is addressed.

Encourage International Cooperation: To tackle global issues like terrorism and climate change, international cooperation is crucial.

Addressing the underlying causes of populism and nationalism will help us move toward a more prosperous and peaceful future.

5.3 The Danger of Cyberattacks and Terrorism

Cyberattacks and terrorism have become major threats to international security in the twenty-first century. These dangers are frequently linked; for example, terrorist activities can be facilitated by cyberattacks, and vice versa.

The act of terrorism

The illegal use of violence and intimidation, particularly against civilians, to further ideological, religious, or political objectives is known as terrorism. To instill fear and cause social unrest, terrorist organizations frequently employ strategies like bombings, kidnappings, and assassinations.

Important Issues Raised by Terrorism:

Death Toll: Terrorist attacks frequently cause a large number of fatalities as well as serious injuries.

Economic Disruption: Terrorist attacks have the potential to harm infrastructure, discourage investment and tourism, and disrupt economic activity.

Political instability: Acts of terrorism have the power to topple governments and erode social harmony.

Psychological Impact: Fear, anxiety, and trauma can result from terrorist attacks, which can have a significant psychological impact on both individuals and societies.

Strategies for Counterterrorism:

Intelligence Sharing: By exchanging intelligence, nations and security organizations can detect and foil terrorist schemes.

Border Security: Improving border security can aid in stopping the flow of terrorists and their supplies.

Counterterrorism Operations: Terrorist groups and their leaders may be the focus of military and law enforcement actions.

Counter-Narrative: The allure of extremist organizations can be diminished by challenging terrorist ideologies and narratives.

International Cooperation: To combat the worldwide threat of terrorism, international cooperation is crucial.

Cyberattacks

Cyberattacks are malevolent actions directed at networks and computer systems. These assaults have the potential to harm economies, steal confidential data, and interfere with vital infrastructure.

Important Cyberattack Types:

Malware is software intended to harm or take down computer systems.
Phishing is the practice of tricking people into disclosing private information, like credit card numbers and passwords.
Malware that encrypts a victim's data and requests a ransom to unlock it is known as ransomware.
DoS (denial-of-service) Attacks: Flooding a target system with traffic in order to deny access to it to authorized users.

Effects of Cyberattacks:

Economic Loss: Businesses and governments may suffer large financial losses as a result of cyberattacks.
Critical Infrastructure Disruption: Cyberattacks have the potential to stop vital services like transportation, water, and electricity.
Data Breaches: Sensitive financial and personal data may be exposed as a result of cyberattacks.

Reputational Damage: Cyberattacks have the potential to harm both individuals' and organizations' reputations.

Techniques for Cybersecurity:

Strong Cybersecurity Measures: Computer systems and networks can be protected by putting in place strong cybersecurity measures like firewalls, intrusion detection systems, and encryption.

Employee Education: It is crucial to teach staff members how to identify and steer clear of online dangers like phishing scams.

Incident Response Plans: Organizations can respond to cyberattacks more successfully if they have a well-developed incident response plan.

International Cooperation: To combat the worldwide threat of cyberattacks, international cooperation is required.

The Relationship Between Cyberattacks and Terrorism

Cyberattacks are being used more and more by terrorist organizations to support their operations. Cyberattacks can be used to launch attacks on vital infrastructure, disseminate propaganda, and recruit new members.

Adopting a comprehensive strategy that integrates law enforcement, cybersecurity, and intelligence sharing is crucial to thwarting the growing threat of terrorism and cyberattacks. Addressing these global issues also requires international cooperation.

Chapter 6:

Pandemics and Health Emergencies

Pandemics and health crises have influenced human history by bringing about social unrest, economic disruption, and widespread suffering. The world has become more interconnected in recent decades, which has facilitated the rapid spread of diseases. This underscores the necessity of strong global health systems and efficient response tactics.

Past Pandemics

Pandemics have decimated populations throughout history.

Among the noteworthy instances are:

Millions of people died during the 14th-century Black Death pandemic that ravaged Europe and Asia due to the bacterium Yersinia pestis.

The Influenza Pandemic of 1918: This pandemic, commonly known as the Spanish flu, killed tens of millions of people and infected an estimated 500 million people globally.

HIV/AIDS: Since its start in the 1980s, the HIV/AIDS pandemic has had a catastrophic effect on world health, especially in Africa.

The pandemic of COVID-19

The SARS-CoV-2 virus, which caused the COVID-19 pandemic, first appeared in late 2019 and spread swiftly throughout the world. It has had a significant effect on economies, societies, and global health.

Principal Effects of COVID-19:

Healthcare Systems Overwhelmed: In many nations, the increase in COVID-19 cases caused a shortage of medical supplies, hospital beds, and healthcare personnel.

Economic Disruption: As a result of company closures, broken supply chains, and skyrocketing unemployment rates, the pandemic caused extensive economic disruption.

Social Disruption: Lockdowns and social distancing policies caused disruptions in day-to-day life, which exacerbated domestic violence, caused mental health problems, and caused isolation.

Rapid Digital Transformation: The pandemic hastened the uptake of digital technologies like telemedicine, online learning, and remote work.

New Health Risks

Global health is at serious risk from a number of new health threats:

Antimicrobial Resistance: The public's health is seriously threatened by the growing number of bacteria that are resistant to antibiotics.

Zoonotic Diseases: Zika and Ebola are two examples of diseases that can spread from animals to people and lead to outbreaks and epidemics.

Climate Change and Health: New diseases may arise as a result of climate change, which may also make pre-existing health issues worse.

Addressing Pandemics and Health Emergencies

A multifaceted strategy is necessary for an effective response to pandemics and health crises:

Strong Public Health Infrastructure: Early outbreak detection and response depend on strong public health infrastructure, which includes surveillance systems, laboratory capacity, and qualified medical personnel.

International Cooperation: Information exchange, response coordination, and the development of vaccines and treatments all depend on international cooperation.

Quick Diagnostic Testing: To identify infected people and control outbreaks, quick and precise diagnostic testing is crucial.

Effective Treatment and Vaccines: Preventing the spread of infectious diseases requires the development of effective treatments and vaccines.

Public Health Messaging: Public education and the promotion of preventive measures can be achieved through clear and consistent public health messaging.

Social and Economic Support: One way to lessen the negative effects of health crises is to offer businesses and individuals social and economic support.

We can improve our readiness and response to future health emergencies by investing in public health infrastructure and learning from previous pandemics.

6.1 Insights from Current Health Emergencies

Recent health emergencies, like the COVID-19 pandemic, have taught us the value of readiness, global collaboration, and fair access to medical care. We can improve our ability to respond to future medical emergencies and fortify our global health systems by taking lessons from these experiences.

The Significance of Being Ready

Being prepared is one of the most important lessons learned from recent health crises. Early detection and quick response to outbreaks depend on having a strong public health infrastructure, which includes reliable surveillance systems, well-stocked labs, and skilled medical personnel.

Early Detection and Response: Timely implementation of control measures depends on early outbreak detection. Both laboratory capacity and robust surveillance systems are necessary for this.

Keeping Medical Supplies in Stock: Responding to outbreaks requires having sufficient supplies of vital medical equipment, such as respirators, masks, and gloves.

Plans for Pandemic Preparedness: Creating thorough plans for pandemic preparedness can assist nations in effectively handling upcoming medical crises.

The Function of Global Collaboration

Addressing global health issues requires international cooperation. Health crises can be lessened by exchanging information, organizing responses, and working together on research and development.

Information Sharing: Monitoring the spread of diseases and putting effective control measures in place depend on timely and accurate information sharing between nations.

Collaborative Research and Development: Effective interventions can be developed more quickly through cooperative efforts to create vaccines, therapies, and diagnostic tests.

Initiatives in Global Health: In order to coordinate global health initiatives and offer countries technical assistance, international organizations like the World Health Organization *(WHO)* are essential.

The necessity of fair access to medical care

Preserving vulnerable populations and halting the spread of infectious diseases require fair access to healthcare.

Universal Health Coverage: Regardless of socioeconomic background, expanding universal health coverage can help guarantee that everyone has access to high-quality medical care.

Resolving Health Disparities: Improving public health outcomes requires addressing health inequities, such as differences in healthcare access depending on socioeconomic status, race, and ethnicity.

Enhancing Primary Healthcare: By preventing and managing illnesses, strengthening primary healthcare systems can lessen the strain on hospitals and other healthcare facilities.

Developing Health Crisis Resilience

In order to increase our ability to withstand future health emergencies, we must:

Invest in Public Health Infrastructure: It is crucial to keep funding public health infrastructure, such as labs, surveillance systems, and the training of medical personnel.

Enhance International Cooperation: Improving international coordination and cooperation can aid in more successfully addressing global health issues.

Encourage Health Equity: Reducing the effects of health crises can be achieved by addressing health disparities and guaranteeing fair access to medical care.

Create Innovative Technologies: Research and development expenditures can result in the creation of novel technologies, including diagnostic instruments, treatments, and vaccines.

Boost Community Involvement: Involving communities in public health initiatives can enhance health outcomes and encourage healthy lifestyle choices.

We can create a healthier, more resilient world and better prepare for and handle future health emergencies by taking lessons from the past and putting these strategies into practice.

6.2 The Value of Infrastructure in Public Health

The foundation of a country's health system is its public health infrastructure, which offers vital services that safeguard and enhance population health. It includes hospitals, clinics, labs, and public health organizations, among many other facilities, systems, and employees. In order to prevent, identify, and address health risks like infectious diseases, chronic illnesses, and natural disasters, a robust public health infrastructure is essential.

Important Elements of the Infrastructure for Public Health

A strong public health infrastructure is made up of various essential elements:

Surveillance Systems: Monitoring population health and identifying infectious disease outbreaks depend on efficient surveillance systems. Data on risk factors and health trends are gathered, examined, and interpreted by these systems.

Laboratory Capacity: Research, disease diagnosis, and the creation of vaccines and treatments all depend on well-equipped labs.

Emergency Response and Preparation: Responding to public health emergencies, including pandemics, natural disasters, and bioterrorism attacks, requires robust emergency preparedness and response systems.

Healthcare Personnel: The provision of high-quality healthcare services depends on a competent and well-trained healthcare workforce, which includes physicians, nurses, and public health specialists.

Essential Public Health Services: In order to prevent illness and promote health, essential public health services like vaccination, maternal and child health, and environmental health are vital.

Public Health Infrastructure's Function in Preventing and Controlling Disease

In order to stop and manage the spread of infectious diseases, public health infrastructure is essential:

Early Detection: By identifying outbreaks early, surveillance systems enable prompt actions to stop their spread.

Quick Response: By putting policies like contact tracing, isolation, and quarantine into place, a well-prepared public health system can react to outbreaks swiftly.

Vaccine Delivery: Vaccines are a vital tool for preventing infectious diseases, and their delivery depends on public health infrastructure.

Health Promotion and Education: To stop the spread of disease, public health campaigns can inform people about healthy habits like washing their hands and getting vaccinated.

Environmental Health: By keeping an eye on the quality of the air and water and encouraging safe food handling techniques, public health organizations can endeavor to enhance environmental health.

The Effects of a Poor Public Health System

Inadequate public health infrastructure can lead to major issues:

Increased Disease Burden: Infectious diseases can spread as a result of insufficient healthcare access and shoddy surveillance systems.

Economic Disruption: Infectious disease outbreaks have the potential to cause economic disruption by resulting in job losses and lower productivity.

Social Disruption: Political instability and social unrest can result from pandemics.

Increased Mortality: Especially for vulnerable populations, a lackluster public health infrastructure can result in higher death rates.

Enhancing the Infrastructure for Public Health

In order to improve the infrastructure for public health, governments and international organizations ought to:

Invest in Public Health: To guarantee that vital services are provided efficiently, public health programs must receive adequate funding.

Create a Skilled Workforce: Developing a strong public health workforce requires funding the education and training of public health professionals.

Encourage International Cooperation: Information exchange, response coordination, and the creation of global health strategies all depend on international cooperation.

Put Equity First: Reducing health disparities and enhancing public health outcomes require equitable access to healthcare services.

Accept Innovation: Public health services can be enhanced by accepting technological advancements like artificial intelligence and digital health tools.

We can safeguard our communities and create a healthier future for everybody if we prioritize preventive measures and invest in public health infrastructure.

6.3 The Function of Technology and Science in the Fight Against Illness

Throughout history, science and technology have been essential in the fight against disease. Scientific discoveries have greatly enhanced human health and prolonged life expectancy, from the creation of vaccines to the improvement of medical therapies.

The Influence of Immunizations

One of the best methods for preventing infectious diseases is vaccination. Vaccines shield people against polio, measles, smallpox, and other diseases by promoting the production of antibodies by the immune system.

Impact on History: Vaccines have eliminated diseases like smallpox and greatly decreased the prevalence of others like measles and polio.

Research Continues: To combat newly emerging and re-emerging diseases, scientists are still working on developing new vaccines.

Obstacles: The emergence of vaccine-resistant strains and the requirement for equitable distribution are obstacles in the development of vaccines.

The Developments in Medical Care

The way we fight diseases has been completely transformed by medical treatments. Numerous lives have been saved by these treatments, which range from chemotherapy to antibiotics.

Antibiotics: The treatment of bacterial infections has benefited greatly from the use of antibiotics. Antibiotic-resistant bacteria, on the other hand, are a serious threat to public health because of the overuse and abuse of antibiotics.

Antiviral medications: These medications work against viruses and can help treat hepatitis C and HIV, among other viral infections.

Chemotherapy: Chemotherapy kills cancer cells in order to treat cancer. Despite its great efficacy, it can have detrimental effects.

Immunotherapy: This kind of cancer treatment works by boosting the body's defenses against cancerous cells.

From the creation of medical devices to the application of artificial intelligence in drug discovery, technology has been instrumental in the fight against disease.

Medical Devices: Medical diagnosis and treatment have been transformed by medical devices like CT scanners, MRI machines, and X-ray machines.

Biotechnology: The creation of novel medications, vaccines, and diagnostic procedures has been made possible by biotechnology.

Artificial Intelligence: AI has the ability to examine enormous volumes of data in order to spot trends and patterns in disease outbreaks. Additionally, it can speed up the development and discovery of new drugs.

Genomics: By shedding light on the genetic causes of illness, genomics has aided in the creation of personalized medicine.

The Effects of International Health Programs

The fight against diseases, especially in low- and middle-income nations, has been greatly aided by global health initiatives. These programs have concentrated on topics like disease surveillance, vaccine development, and bolstering health systems.

Billions of dollars have been invested in the fight against AIDS, tuberculosis, and malaria through the Global Fund to Fight These Diseases.

The GAVI Alliance: GAVI helps save millions of lives by funding immunization programs in low-income nations.

The WHO, or World Health Organization: In order to respond to outbreaks, coordinate international health initiatives, and establish global health standards, the WHO is essential.

Obstacles and Prospects

The battle against disease still faces obstacles despite tremendous advancements. These difficulties include antibiotic resistance, the rise of new illnesses, and unequal access to medical care.

Emerging Diseases: The rise of novel illnesses like COVID-19 emphasizes the necessity of ongoing monitoring and prompt action.

Antimicrobial Resistance: The creation of novel antibiotics and the encouragement of antibiotic stewardship are imperative due to the growing threat posed by bacteria that are resistant to antibiotics.

Global Health Equity: Global health security depends on ensuring fair access to healthcare, especially in low- and middle-income nations.

We can overcome these obstacles and create a healthier future for everybody if we keep funding research, innovation, and global health programs.

Part III:
A Path Forward

Chapter 7:

Entrepreneurship and Innovation: Fueling Economic Development

Technological advancements, job creation, and societal progress are all fueled by innovation and entrepreneurship. In the current dynamic global economy, these two factors are more important than ever.

Innovation's Power

The process of introducing novel concepts, procedures, or goods is referred to as innovation. Because it boosts competitiveness, efficiency, and productivity, it is essential to economic growth. From ground-breaking scientific discoveries to small-scale enhancements of already existing goods and services, innovation can take many different forms.

Important forces behind innovation:

Research and Development (R&D): To spur innovation, R&D spending is essential. It enables companies and organizations to develop new technologies, produce new goods, and investigate novel concepts.

Rights to Intellectual Property: Strong intellectual property rights, like copyrights and patents, safeguard creators and encourage more innovation.

Training and Education: Innovation requires a workforce with a high level of education. Programs for education and training can give people the abilities and information required to innovate.

Taking Chances and Trying New Things: Innovation is fostered by a culture that values experimentation and taking risks. Businesses and governments can promote this culture by providing funding sources and enacting laws that encourage it.

The Function of Entrepreneurship

The process of establishing and managing a business is known as entrepreneurship. Entrepreneurs take chances, spot opportunities, and launch new businesses. By fostering innovation, producing wealth, and creating jobs, they are essential to economic growth.

Important Qualities of Successful Business Owners:

Innovation: Successful businesspeople frequently have fresh concepts and methods.
Risk-Taking: Entrepreneurs aren't afraid to invest in their businesses and take chances.
Perseverance: In the face of difficulties, entrepreneurs need to be resilient and persistent.
Leadership: Establishing and running a profitable company requires strong leadership abilities.
The Confluence of Entrepreneurship and Innovation

Entrepreneurship and innovation are closely related. By bringing new concepts and technologies to market, entrepreneurs frequently spur innovation. In a similar vein, innovation can open doors for business owners to launch new ventures.

Important Techniques for Promoting Entrepreneurship and Innovation:

Government Policies: Through grants, tax breaks, and regulatory changes, governments can encourage entrepreneurship and innovation.

Education and Training: Funding educational initiatives can contribute to the creation of a workforce with the necessary skills.

Financial Access: For entrepreneurs to launch and expand their companies, financial resources like loans and venture capital are essential.

Mentoring and Networking: These programs can assist business owners in honing their abilities and making connections with possible partners and investors.

Intellectual Property Protection: By defending the rights of creators and inventors, robust intellectual property protection can promote innovation.

Innovation and Entrepreneurship's Future

With the help of cutting-edge technologies like blockchain, biotechnology, and artificial intelligence, innovation and entrepreneurship have a bright future. These technologies have the power to transform entire sectors and open up fresh business prospects for entrepreneurs. But obstacles like inequality, climate change, and geopolitical tensions could impede development.

It is crucial to keep encouraging innovation and entrepreneurship in order to guarantee a sustainable and prosperous future. We can unleash the full potential of human creativity and ingenuity by making investments in infrastructure, research, and education as well as by fostering an environment that is conducive to business.

7.1 The role of innovation in driving progress

Throughout history, innovation—the act of presenting novel concepts, procedures, or goods—has acted as a spur for human advancement. Innovation has influenced economies, societies, and cultures since the wheel's invention to the creation of artificial intelligence. Innovation is more important than ever in the quickly evolving world of today to solve global issues and promote sustainable development.

Innovation's Effect on Society

Society has greatly benefited from innovation, which has produced notable breakthroughs in a number of fields:

Economic Growth: By generating new industries, jobs, and wealth, innovation propels economic growth.

Better Quality of Life: Technological, medical, and agricultural advancements have greatly raised people's standard of living.

Social Progress: Innovation can help solve social problems like inequality, poverty, and climate change.

Important Forces Behind Innovation

Innovation is influenced by several factors, including:

Research and Development (R&D): To spur innovation, R&D spending is essential. It enables companies and organizations to develop new technologies, produce new goods, and investigate novel concepts.

Education and Training: Innovation requires a workforce with a high level of education. Programs for education and training can give people the abilities and information required to innovate.

Intellectual Property Rights: Robust intellectual property rights, like copyrights and patents, safeguard pioneers and encourage more innovation.

Entrepreneurship: By bringing new concepts and technologies to market, entrepreneurs significantly contribute to the advancement of innovation.

Government Policies: By offering financial incentives, regulatory frameworks, and other resources, government policies can foster innovation.

Technology's Place in Innovation

Innovation has accelerated due to technological advancements. Emerging technologies like biotechnology, nanotechnology, and artificial intelligence have the power to transform a number of industries and provide solutions to challenging global issues.

Artificial Intelligence (AI): AI is capable of intelligent decision-making, task automation, and large-scale dataset analysis.

Biotechnology: Biotechnology has the power to completely transform environmental science, agriculture, and healthcare.

Nanotechnology: Creating new materials and gadgets through the manipulation of matter at the atomic and molecular level is known as nanotechnology.

Opportunities and Difficulties

Innovation has enormous potential, but there are drawbacks as well.

Among the main difficulties are:

Ethical Considerations: Concerns about privacy, security, and employment effects are among the ethical issues brought up by the creation and application of new technologies.

Inequality: If innovation is not available to everyone, inequality may worsen.

Environmental Impact: Technology use and production may have an adverse effect on the environment.

Promoting responsible innovation and making sure that everyone benefits from it are crucial in addressing these issues.

7.2 The importance of supporting entrepreneurship

The process of launching and operating a business, or entrepreneurship, is a key driver of innovation, job creation, and economic growth. Governments, corporations, and people can promote economic growth and raise living standards by creating an atmosphere that is encouraging to entrepreneurs.

The Effects of Entrepreneurship on the Economy

A key factor in promoting economic development and growth is entrepreneurship.

Job Creation: Both directly and indirectly, entrepreneurs generate jobs. Businesses hire staff as they expand, creating more job opportunities.

Innovation: Creating new goods, services, and business models puts entrepreneurs frequently at the forefront of innovation. This promotes competitiveness and economic growth.

Economic Development: Local economies can be revived by entrepreneurship, especially in underserved and rural areas. Entrepreneurs can support economic growth by starting companies and making investments in their local communities.

The Effects of Entrepreneurship on Society

In addition to its financial advantages, entrepreneurship can have a big social impact.

Social Change: Entrepreneurs have the ability to solve social issues and bring about constructive social change. Social entrepreneurs, for instance, might concentrate on problems like environmental sustainability, education, and poverty.

Community Development: By establishing jobs, funding regional infrastructure, and lending support to regional nonprofits, entrepreneurs can help their communities grow.

Empowerment: By giving people the chance to become financially independent and self-sufficient, entrepreneurship can empower people, especially women and marginalized groups.

Obstacles Entrepreneurs Face

Notwithstanding the possible advantages, entrepreneurs encounter many difficulties:

Access to Finance: For entrepreneurs, obtaining capital can be a major challenge, particularly for startups.

Regulatory Obstacles: Bureaucratic obstacles and complicated regulations can impede a company's ability to expand.

Lack of Business Knowledge and Skills: Many entrepreneurs might not have the knowledge and skills needed to be successful in the business world.

Market Uncertainty: Businesses may experience uncertainty as a result of economic downturns, shifting consumer preferences, and heightened competition.

Encouragement of Entrepreneurship

There are various actions that governments, corporations, and individuals can take to encourage entrepreneurship:

Government Policies: By enacting laws that cut red tape, offer tax breaks, and fund education and training, governments can foster an atmosphere that is conducive to entrepreneurship.

Financial Support: For entrepreneurs, having access to funding is essential. To assist new businesses, governments and financial institutions can offer grants, loans, and equity financing.

Mentoring and Coaching: Programs for mentoring and coaching can assist business owners in expanding their knowledge and skill sets.

Incubators and Accelerators: These organizations give business owners access to resources, networking opportunities, and mentorship.

Education and Training: Programs for education and training can support the growth of entrepreneurial knowledge and abilities.

Cultural Support: A flourishing entrepreneurial ecosystem can be fostered by a culture that values innovation, entrepreneurship, and taking risks.

We can build a more prosperous and just future for everybody if we encourage entrepreneurship.

7.2 The Gig Economy and the Future of Work

Technology breakthroughs, globalization, and shifting social values are all having a major impact on the nature of work in the future. The traditional model of employment is changing due to the emergence of the gig economy, which is defined by flexible, short-term work arrangements.

The Development of Work

The nature of work has changed over time. Every era, from prehistoric times to the Industrial Revolution and the Information Age, has presented its own special opportunities and problems. Another big change is taking place in the twenty-first century as globalization and technology change how we work.

The Gig Economy's Ascent

The gig economy is defined by flexible, temporary work schedules. Gig workers are independent contractors who work on a project-by-project basis. They frequently communicate with clients via digital platforms.

Important Elements Fueling the Gig Economy:

Technological Developments: People can now more easily locate and connect with employment opportunities thanks to digital platforms.
Changing Workforce Demographics: More and more people are looking for flexible work schedules, especially Gen Z and millennials.

Economic Uncertainty: More people are turning to gig work as a source of income as a result of job insecurity and economic downturns.

A few advantages of the gig economy are

Flexibility: Gig workers are free to set their own schedules and work on several projects at once.

Autonomy: Gig workers are able to determine their own prices and have more control over their work.

Possibility of Entrepreneurship: The gig economy can provide a platform for business owners to test out new concepts and launch ventures.

The gig economy's challenges include:

Job Insecurity: Gig workers may experience changes in their income and frequently lack job security.

Absence of Benefits: Gig workers might not be eligible for paid time off, retirement plans, or health insurance.

Implications for Law and Taxation: Gig work can have complicated legal and tax ramifications that differ from nation to nation.

Work in the Future: A Hybrid Approach

A hybrid work model that combines gig work and traditional employment is probably the way of the future. Employees can now work remotely or part-time thanks to the widespread adoption of flexible work arrangements by many organizations.

Important Trends Affecting the Future of Employment:

Remote Work: As technology makes it possible for workers to work from any location, remote work is growing in popularity.

AI and automation: These two technologies are revolutionizing industries, displacing workers and creating new positions.

Reskilling and Upskilling: In order to stay competitive as the labor market changes, workers will need to constantly reskill and upskill.

Soft Skills Are Essential: In the workplace of the future, soft skills like problem-solving, creativity, and communication will be more and more crucial.

The Function of Companies and Governments

Businesses and governments have a significant impact on how work is shaped in the future. Governments can enact laws that help gig economy workers by giving them access to healthcare benefits and social safety nets. Companies can invest in staff training and development, establish flexible work schedules, and promote an innovative and adaptable culture.

It is evident that the conventional model of employment is changing, even though the future of work is unclear. We can build a more adaptable, just, and sustainable workplace of the future by seizing the opportunities and tackling the problems presented by the gig economy.

Chapter 8:

Lifelong Learning and Education: A Basis for the Future

Both individual and societal advancement depend on education and lifelong learning. They enable people to develop the values, abilities, and knowledge necessary to fulfill their potential and give back to their communities.

The Value of Education

The foundation of human development is education. It gives people the resources they need to comprehend the world, find solutions to issues, and come to wise decisions.

A good education can:

Encourage Economic Growth: Innovation and economic growth depend on a workforce with a high level of education.

Reduce Poverty: By equipping people with the abilities and information required to land decent jobs, education can aid in the reduction of poverty.

Enhance Health: Education can raise awareness of health risks and encourage healthy habits like good diet and hygiene.

Encourage Social Cohesion: By encouraging tolerance, respect for diversity, and understanding, education can aid in the development of social cohesion.

The Significance of Continuous Education

Lifelong learning is crucial for people to stay competitive and adjust to new challenges in the quickly evolving world of today. Continuous learning and skill development throughout one's life are components of lifelong learning.

Principal Advantages of Lifelong Learning:

Increased Employability: People can become more employable in the labor market by acquiring new skills and knowledge through lifelong learning.

Greater Earning Potential: People who have received more education and training typically make more money.

Personal Satisfaction: By broadening one's knowledge and perspectives, lifelong learning can improve people's quality of life.

Social and Civic Engagement: Active citizenship and community involvement can be fostered by lifelong learning.

Obstacles to Lifelong Learning and Education

Despite the value of education and lifelong learning, advancement is hampered by a number of issues:

Access Inequality: Not everyone, especially in developing nations, has equal access to high-quality education.

Financial Restraints: For many people, the expense of education, particularly higher education, can be a major obstacle.

__Lack of Knowledge:__ A lot of people don't know how to access learning opportunities or the advantages of lifelong learning.

__Digital Divide:__ The digital divide may restrict access to opportunities and resources for online learning.

Education's Future

Both shifting societal demands and technological developments will probably influence education in the future.

Among the major trends are:

__Online Learning:__ People can now more easily access training and education thanks to online learning platforms.

__Personalized Learning:__ Personalized learning strategies can adjust instruction to each student's unique requirements and preferred method of learning.

__Artificial Intelligence:__ AI can improve teaching and learning, automate administrative duties, and personalize learning experiences.

Lifelong Learning as the Norm: As technology advances at an accelerated rate, lifelong learning will become more and more significant.

Education and lifelong learning are vital investments for a bright future. We can build a more just, prosperous, and sustainable world by giving everyone access to high-quality education and training opportunities.

8.1 The necessity of flexible educational frameworks

The conventional educational system is confronted with previously unheard-of difficulties in the quickly evolving world of today. Education systems must become more flexible and responsive to the changing demands of society if they are to prepare students for the future.

The Changing Educational Environment

The need for flexible educational systems is being driven by a number of factors:

Technological Advancements: Industries are changing and new job opportunities are being created by the quick speed of technological innovation. For students to succeed in this new era, educational systems must give them the digital skills and critical thinking abilities they need.

Globalization: As a result of globalization, there is now more competition and connectivity. Students must acquire intercultural competency and global citizenship skills in order to compete in the global economy.

Climate Change: Both society and the environment face serious challenges as a result of climate change. Students must be prepared by their educational systems to handle these issues and create a sustainable future.

Social and Economic Inequality: By giving every student the chance to realize their full potential, education can significantly contribute to the reduction of inequality.

Essential Elements of Flexible Educational Frameworks

Education systems need to be responsive, flexible, and adaptive to meet these challenges.

Among the essential characteristics of flexible educational systems are:

Customizing instruction to meet each student's unique needs and learning preferences is known as personalized learning.

Flexible Learning Environments: Providing a range of learning settings, including blended learning, online learning, and traditional classrooms.

Lifelong Learning: Encouraging opportunities for lifelong learning to keep people up to date with new trends and technological developments.

Giving pupils the digital skills they need to function in the digital age is known as digital literacy.

Developing students' critical thinking and problem-solving abilities will help them to evaluate complicated problems and come up with creative answers.

Creativity and Innovation: Encouraging students to think creatively and innovatively will help them generate new ideas.

Global Citizenship: Fostering intercultural understanding and a sense of global citizenship. Teaching students about sustainable practices and environmental issues is known as environmental education.

Opportunities and Difficulties

Even though the necessity of flexible educational systems is becoming more widely acknowledged, there are still a number of obstacles to overcome:

Training and Development for Teachers: Teachers must possess the abilities and know-how to provide efficient instruction in a range of learning settings.

Technology Integration: Teachers may need more assistance and training when integrating technology into the classroom, which can be difficult.

Equity and Access: One of the biggest challenges is making sure that everyone has fair access to high-quality education, especially for underserved populations.

There are plenty of chances to revolutionize education in spite of these obstacles. We can design educational systems that equip students for the opportunities and challenges of the twenty-first century by embracing technology, encouraging innovation, and placing a high priority on student-centered learning.

The Function of Authorities and Teachers

The future of education is greatly influenced by governments and educators. Governments have the power to fund education, create laws that encourage it, and provide funds to educational institutions. Teachers can use creative teaching strategies, encourage critical thinking, and cultivate a passion for learning. Communities, educators, and governments can collaborate to develop educational systems that meet the demands of the twenty-first century.

8.2 The Value of Problem-Solving and Critical Thinking Ability

Critical thinking and problem-solving skills are more crucial than ever in the quickly evolving world of today. Success in school, the workplace, and personal life all depend on these abilities.

Critical thinking: what is it?

Analyzing data, assessing supporting evidence, and drawing logical conclusions are all components of critical thinking. People must challenge presumptions, take into account various viewpoints, and make well-informed decisions.

Crucial Elements of Critical Thought:

Analysis: Dividing intricate data into manageable chunks in order to comprehend the fundamental ideas.

Evaluation: Determining the veracity and applicability of data.

Inference: Making judgments based on logic and supporting data.

Problem-Solving: recognizing issues, coming up with fixes, and assessing how well those fixes work.

Creativity: The ability to think creatively and innovatively in order to generate novel concepts and methods.

The Value of Problem-Solving Capabilities

Critical thinking and problem-solving abilities are closely related. They entail the capacity to recognize and characterize issues, come up with solutions, and put those solutions into action.

Important Steps in Solving Problems:

Determine the issue: Clearly state the issue and its underlying causes.

Provide Solutions: Come up with a number of different ways to solve the issue.

Evaluate Solutions: Consider each solution's viability, efficacy, and possible repercussions.

Put the Solution into Practice: Decide on the best option and put it into action.

Analyze the result: Evaluate the solution's efficacy and make any necessary modifications.

The Advantages of Problem-Solving and Critical Thinking Skills

Numerous advantages can result from having strong critical thinking and problem-solving abilities, such as:

Enhanced Academic Performance: These abilities are critical for academic and postsecondary success.

Improved Career Opportunities: Critical thinkers and problem solvers are highly valued by employers.

Improved Decision-Making: These abilities can assist people in making well-informed choices in both their personal and professional lives.

Enhanced Creativity and Innovation: New ideas and creative solutions can result from critical thinking and problem-solving.

Effective Communication: Collaboration and communication can be enhanced by having strong critical thinking and problem-solving abilities.

How to Improve Your Ability to Think Critically and Solve Problems

The following are some methods for honing these crucial abilities:

Encourage curiosity by raising questions about everything.

Challenge Assumptions: Analyze information critically rather than accepting things at face value.

Seek Diverse Viewpoints: Take into account various points of view.

Engage in active listening by paying attention to the thoughts and viewpoints of others.

Collaborative Problem-Solving: Solve issues and come up with fresh concepts by working with others.

Request Feedback: Get input on your work from others and be receptive to helpful criticism.

Read widely: You can be exposed to a variety of viewpoints and ideas by reading books, articles, and news reports.

Play games: These abilities can be developed by playing games that require strategy and problem-solving.

People can become better workers, citizens, and learners by honing their critical thinking and problem-solving abilities. Navigating the complexity of the twenty-first century and building a better future require these abilities.

8.3 Lifelong Learning's Significance in a Changing World

The idea of lifelong learning has grown in significance in the quickly changing world of today. The capacity to continuously learn and adapt is essential for both individuals and organizations as societal demands, industries, and technology change. People who pursue lifelong learning are better equipped to stay current, pick up new skills, and make significant contributions to society.

The Significance of Lifelong Learning

There are various reasons why lifelong learning is crucial.

Adaptability to Change: Lifelong learning helps people adjust to new technologies, work procedures, and social trends in a world that is changing quickly.

Improved Career Prospects: Ongoing education can result in job security, higher earning potential, and career advancement.

Personal Development: Lifelong learning can promote personal development, resulting in enhanced critical thinking abilities, creativity, and self-assurance.

Social and Civic Engagement: By giving people the information and abilities to take part in their communities, lifelong learning can improve social and civic engagement.

Economic Growth: Innovation, productivity, and economic growth can be stimulated by a population that is actively involved in lifelong learning.

The Advantages of Continuous Education

There are many advantages to lifelong learning, such as:

Enhanced Knowledge and Skills: People can broaden their knowledge and pick up new skills by learning new things on a regular basis.

Better Problem-Solving Skills: Critical thinking and problem-solving abilities can be improved through lifelong learning.

Enhanced Creativity: Innovation and creativity can be sparked by exposure to fresh viewpoints and ideas.

Enhanced Confidence: Gaining new knowledge can increase one's sense of self-worth and confidence.

Better Career Opportunities: Career advancement and higher earning potential can result from lifelong learning.

Techniques for Continuous Education

Individuals can embrace lifelong learning in a number of ways, including:

Formal Education: Getting a master's or doctoral degree can help you gain advanced knowledge and skills.

Informal Learning: Online courses, workshops, and book reading are just a few examples of the various ways that people can learn informally.

Mentoring and Coaching: Consulting with mentors and coaches can yield insightful advice and helpful support.

Networking: Establishing and preserving robust professional networks can open doors to cooperation and education.

Experiential Learning: Gaining practical skills and knowledge through practical experiences, like volunteering or internships, can be very beneficial.

Digital Learning: Accessible and adaptable learning opportunities are provided by online learning platforms.

Technology's Place in Lifelong Learning

Technology has completely changed how we learn. Numerous learning opportunities are provided by virtual reality, smartphone apps, and online learning platforms.

Online Courses: Access to education is made flexible and reasonably priced through online courses.

Mobile Learning: People can learn while on the go thanks to mobile devices, which increases accessibility to education.

Virtual and Augmented Reality: Immersion technologies have the potential to improve and increase the engagement of learning.

Lifelong Learning's Future

Lifelong learning has a promising future, and technology will only become more significant. The need for lifelong learning will only increase as the world changes. People can accomplish their goals, adjust to change, and help create a better future by embracing lifelong learning.

Chapter 9:

Sustainable Development and Environmental Stewardship

The idea of sustainable development aims to strike a balance between environmental preservation, social justice, and economic growth. It seeks to satisfy current needs without endangering the capacity of future generations to satisfy their own. Because it entails taking responsible care of the environment, environmental stewardship is an essential part of sustainable development.

The Economy, Society, and Environment Are Linked

The environment, society, and economy are all intertwined. Economic activity can have a big impact on the environment and frequently depends on natural resources. Sustainable development requires social equity because it guarantees that everyone has access to the tools and chances they require to prosper.

Essential Elements of Sustainable Development

A number of fundamental ideas form the foundation of the idea of sustainable development:

Ensuring that future generations have equal access to resources and opportunities as the current generation is known as intergenerational equity.
Fairly allocating the advantages and costs of development within the present generation is known as intragenerational equity.
The precautionary principle is the practice of taking preventative measures when it is unclear whether a given activity will have unfavorable effects.
The Polluter Pays Principle holds the polluter accountable for the expenses incurred as a result of environmental harm.

Environmental Stewardship Being an environmental steward means caring for and protecting the environment.

This comprises:

Natural resource conservation is the process of safeguarding resources like forests, water, and wildlife in order to maintain their sustainability over the long run.

Preventing and controlling pollution involves cutting back on waste and pollution to lessen harm to the environment.

Reducing greenhouse gas emissions and lessening the effects of climate change is known as climate change mitigation.

Conserving ecosystems and biodiversity is known as biodiversity conservation.

Sustainable Agriculture: Encouraging sustainable farming methods to lessen their negative effects on the environment and guarantee food security.

The Function of People and Institutions

Promoting environmental stewardship and sustainable development is a critical responsibility of both individuals and organizations.

Among the ways to help are:

Conserving resources and lessening the impact on the environment can be achieved by reducing waste, reusing products, and recycling materials.

Conserving Water and Energy: Conserving water and energy can help preserve water supplies and lower greenhouse gas emissions.

Supporting Sustainable Businesses: You can promote sustainable practices by purchasing goods from businesses that place a high priority on sustainability.

Volunteering: Supporting sustainable development and environmental protection can be achieved by volunteering for environmental organizations.

Advocacy: One way to contribute to a more sustainable future is to advocate for laws that support sustainability.

Opportunities and Difficulties

Even though sustainable development has made great strides, there are still many obstacles to overcome.

Among the main difficulties are:

Economic Growth and Environmental Protection: Striking the correct balance between environmental protection and economic growth is a difficult undertaking.

Addressing Climate Change: The environment and human society are seriously threatened by climate change.

Poverty and Inequality: Attempts to promote sustainable development may be hampered by poverty and inequality.

On the other hand, there are plenty of chances to build a more sustainable future. We can endeavor to create a more sustainable and just world by adopting cutting-edge technologies, encouraging eco-friendly behaviors, and cultivating global collaboration.

Maintaining a healthy planet and a prosperous future depend on environmental stewardship and sustainable development. We can make wise decisions and take action to safeguard our planet if we comprehend how economic, social, and environmental factors are interconnected.

9.1 Keeping Environmental Protection and Economic Growth in Check

For many years, businesses and policymakers have faced the difficult task of striking a balance between environmental preservation and economic growth. The strain on ecosystems and natural resources increases as economies around the world continue to grow. Adopting laws and procedures that support economic expansion and reduce environmental damage is essential to ensuring sustainable development.

The Economic and Environmental Interdependencies

The environment and the economy are closely intertwined. Resources that are vital to economic activity, such as clean water, air, and fertile land, are provided by a healthy environment. On the other hand, economic operations like transportation and industrial production can harm the environment by causing pollution, deforestation, and climate change.

Finding a Balance: Crucial Techniques for Sustainable Development

Development that satisfies current needs without jeopardizing the capacity of future generations to satisfy their own needs is known as sustainable development.

Implementation: striking a balance between environmental preservation, social justice, and economic growth.

Important Guidelines:

Making sure that future generations have the same opportunities as the present generation is known as intergenerational equity.
Equitable distribution of the advantages and costs of economic expansion within the present generation is known as intragenerational equity. The precautionary principle is the practice of taking preventative measures when it is unclear whether a given activity will have unfavorable effects.

Innovation and Clean Technologies:

Investing in R&D: Promoting clean technology research and development can result in innovations in energy efficiency, pollution prevention, and renewable energy.

Encouraging Innovation: The development of sustainable technologies can be aided by establishing an environment that is favorable to innovation, such as through tax breaks and the protection of intellectual property.

Adopting Clean Technologies: Greenhouse gas emissions and other pollutants can be decreased by promoting the use of clean technologies, such as solar energy and electric cars.

The circular economy

Reducing, Reusing, and Recycling: Encouraging a circular economy, in which waste is reduced and resources are used effectively, can help lessen the impact on the environment.

Increasing Product Lifespans: By making products durable and repairable, waste disposal and new production can be minimized.

Recycling and Upcycling: Promoting recycling and upcycling can help cut down on pollution and save resources.

Ecological Production and Consumption:

Promoting Sustainable Consumption: One way to lessen the impact on the environment is to encourage consumers to make sustainable decisions, such as purchasing locally produced goods and cutting back on waste.

Sustainable Production Practices: Businesses can lessen their environmental impact by promoting sustainable production practices, such as cutting back on energy and water use.

Environmental Standards and Regulations:

Tight Environmental Regulations: To protect the environment and hold polluters responsible, stringent environmental regulations should be put into place and enforced.

International Collaboration: Achieving sustainable development goals can be facilitated by working with other nations to address global environmental issues like biodiversity loss and climate change.

Opportunities and Difficulties

It's difficult to strike a balance between environmental preservation and economic growth.

Among the main difficulties are:

Long-term vs. Short-term Gains: Long-term environmental sustainability may suffer in order to achieve short-term financial gains.

Managing Conflicting Interests: It can be challenging to manage the interests of various stakeholders, including companies, customers, and environmental organizations.

Absence of Political Will: In order to execute successful environmental policies, there must be a strong political will.

But there are also plenty of chances to attain sustainable development. We can build a future where environmental preservation and economic prosperity coexist by supporting sustainable practices, investing in clean technologies, and embracing creative solutions.

9.2 Sustainable Consumption and the Circular Economy

Sharing, renting, reusing, repairing, refurbishing, and recycling existing materials and products for as long as possible are all part of the circular economy model of production and consumption. The circular economy seeks to maximize resource efficiency and reduce waste, in contrast to the conventional linear economy, which operates on a *"take-make-dispose"* basis. A key component of the circular economy is sustainable consumption, which encourages customers to make thoughtful decisions that lessen their impact on the environment.

Important Circular Economy Principles

Environmental Design: Products are made with end-of-life considerations in mind, taking durability, repairability, and recycling into account.

Sharing Economy: By pooling resources and goods, individual ownership and consumption may be less necessary.

Product Lifecycle Extension: Increasing a product's lifespan by repairing, reusing, and refurbishing it.

Reusing materials to make new products and upcycling them to make more valuable products are two examples of recycling and upcycling.

Utilizing renewable energy sources to drive both production and consumption is known as renewable energy.

Sustainable Consumption's Function

Making thoughtful decisions that reduce your impact on the environment is a key component of sustainable consumption.

In order to support the circular economy, consumers can:

Cutting back on consumption means avoiding pointless purchases and only purchasing what is required.

Selecting Sustainable Products: Choosing long-lasting, energy-efficient, and sustainably produced goods.

Repairing and Reusing: Whenever feasible, repair damaged items rather than throwing them away.

Recycling and Composting: To cut down on waste and preserve resources, recycle materials and compost food scraps.

Supporting Sustainable Businesses: Assisting companies that place a high value on ethics and sustainability.

Advantages of Sustainable Consumption and the Circular Economy

Benefits to the environment include less waste, pollution, and depletion of resources.

Economic benefits include cost savings, economic expansion, and job creation.

Social Benefits: Better social well-being, less inequality, and better public health.

Opportunities and Difficulties

Notwithstanding the many advantages, there are a number of obstacles to promoting sustainable consumption and putting the circular economy into practice:

Technology and Infrastructure: It can be expensive and difficult to develop the technologies and infrastructure required to support a circular economy.

Consumer Behavior: Education and awareness campaigns are necessary to alter consumer behavior and promote sustainable consumption practices.

Policy and Regulation: In order to encourage the circular economy and deter unsustainable practices, government policies and regulations can be extremely important.

There are, nevertheless, also plenty of chances to quicken the shift to a circular economy.

These consist of:

Innovation and Technology: New ideas for resource efficiency, waste reduction, and sustainable production can be made possible by technological developments.

Cooperation and Partnerships: To propel the shift to a circular economy, cooperation between governments, corporations, and consumers is crucial.

Education and Awareness: Spreading knowledge of the advantages of the circular economy and encouraging sustainable consumption can motivate people to take constructive action.

We can build a more resilient and sustainable future for future generations by adopting the circular economy's tenets and engaging in sustainable consumption.

9.3 The Function of Global Collaboration

Addressing global issues that cut across national boundaries requires international cooperation. Countries can share knowledge, pool resources, and execute coordinated solutions to challenging issues by cooperating.

The Value of International Cooperation in

Addressing Global Challenges: Addressing global issues like poverty, disease, and climate change requires international cooperation.

Encouraging Peace and Security: International collaboration can aid in averting wars and fostering peace.

Promoting Economic Growth: Through trade, investment, and the sharing of technologies, international cooperation can promote economic growth.

Knowledge and Expertise Sharing: In fields like science, technology, and education, nations can gain from exchanging knowledge and expertise.

Important Domains for Global Collaboration

Climate Change: Reducing greenhouse gas emissions, preparing for the effects of climate change, and funding climate action all require international cooperation.

Global Health: In order to respond to pandemics and other global health emergencies and to advance public health programs, international cooperation is essential.

Trade and Investment: Agreements pertaining to international trade and investment have the potential to foster economic expansion.

Security: To tackle global security issues like cybercrime, terrorism, and nuclear proliferation, international cooperation is crucial.

Humanitarian Aid: In order to provide humanitarian aid to those impacted by poverty, conflicts, and disasters, international cooperation is essential.

Obstacles to Global Collaboration

Despite its significance, there are a number of obstacles to international cooperation:

National Interests: Disagreements and tensions between nations can arise when national interests clash with global interests.

Political Differences: International cooperation may be hampered by disparities in political philosophies and systems of government.

Economic Inequality: Power and influence imbalances can result from economic differences between nations.

Cultural Differences: Misunderstandings and poor communication can occasionally result from cultural differences.

Strengthening Global Collaboration

Several tactics can be used to get past these obstacles and improve global cooperation:

Diplomatic Engagement: In order to settle conflicts and foster international trust, diplomatic communication and negotiations are crucial.

International Organizations: Promoting international cooperation is greatly aided by international organizations like the World Trade Organization and the United Nations.

Multilateralism: When it comes to tackling global issues, multilateral cooperation—which involves several nations—can be more successful than bilateral cooperation.

Public diplomacy: This tactic can promote mutual respect and understanding between countries.

Civil Society Engagement: By influencing public opinion and pushing for particular policies, civil society organizations can be extremely helpful in advancing global cooperation.

Tackling the intricate problems the world is currently facing requires international cooperation. Nations can build a more sustainable, prosperous, and peaceful future by cooperating.

Chapter 10:

Equity and Social Justice

A just and equitable society is based on the core ideas of social justice and equity. They speak of a society's equitable allocation of resources, opportunities, and privileges. Ensuring that everyone has equal rights and opportunities, irrespective of their gender, race, class, or other social identities, is a key component of social justice. Conversely, equity emphasizes impartiality and fairness.

The Value of Equity and Social Justice

Equity and social justice are crucial for a number of reasons:

Encouraging Human Rights: Social justice guarantees the protection and observance of everyone's human rights.

Reducing Inequality: Social justice can contribute to poverty reduction and the enhancement of marginalized groups' quality of life by tackling systemic inequalities.

Creating Strong Communities: Communities that are inclusive, resilient, and strong are fostered by social justice.

Encouraging Social Harmony: Social justice can lessen social conflict by tackling issues of discrimination and injustice.

Ensuring that everyone has the chance to contribute to the economy is one way that a just and equitable society can encourage economic growth.

Obstacles to Equity and Social Justice

Even with great advancements, there are still many obstacles in the way of attaining equity and social justice.

Among the main difficulties are:

Systemic Discrimination: Racism, sexism, and classism are examples of systemic discrimination that can restrict opportunities and maintain inequality.

Economic Inequality: Social and political instability can result from economic inequality.

Lack of Resources: A lot of people, especially those from underrepresented groups, might not have access to basic resources like housing, healthcare, and education.

Political Polarization: When it comes to social justice issues, political polarization can impede progress.

Global Inequality: Social and economic inequalities are made worse by global inequality, both between and within nations.

Methods for Advancement of Equity and Social Justice

Several tactics can be used to address these issues and advance equity and social justice:

Education and Awareness: Education can support empathy, dispel stereotypes, and cultivate a respectful and tolerant society.

Reforming policies: Progressive taxation, universal healthcare, and affordable housing are a few examples of measures that governments can put into place to address systemic injustices.

Social Activism: Social movements and activism have the power to inspire people to demand change and increase public awareness of social issues.

International Cooperation: Addressing global inequality and advancing human rights can be accomplished through international cooperation.

Community Engagement: People can be empowered to solve local problems and strengthen their communities through community engagement.

Individuals' Role

People can significantly contribute to the advancement of equity and social justice by:

Educating Oneself: Acquiring knowledge of social justice concerns and comprehending the underlying causes of inequality.

Volunteering: Contributing to groups that advance equity and social justice.

Contributing to Social Causes: Assisting groups that are tackling social issues.

Speaking out against injustice and supporting laws that advance equity are two ways to advocate for change.

Empathy and Compassion Practice: Having empathy and compassion for other people, particularly those who are underprivileged or marginalized.

Together, people and societies can make the world more fair and just for everybody.

10.1 Resolving Systemic Disparities

Disparities in opportunities and results for various groups are sustained by systemic inequalities, which have their roots in society's institutions and structures. These disparities may be racial, gender, socioeconomic, or geographic, among other manifestations. A multifaceted strategy involving people, communities, organizations, and governments is needed to address these systemic problems.

Comprehending Systemic Inequality

Systemic inequality is ingrained in institutions and societal structures rather than being solely the product of personal biases or prejudices. It can be sustained by norms, policies, and practices that discriminate against particular groups, whether on purpose or accidentally.

Systemic inequality frequently appears in the following important areas:

Education: Inequalities can be maintained and opportunities restricted by unequal access to high-quality education.
Healthcare: Inequalities in marginalized groups' access to healthcare can result in worse health outcomes.
Employment: Certain groups may have fewer economic opportunities if they are subjected to discrimination in hiring, promotion, and pay.

Criminal Justice System: Disproportionate incarceration rates for particular groups may result from biases in the criminal justice system. *Housing:* Access to safe and reasonably priced housing may be restricted due to discrimination in the housing industry.

Methods for Dealing with Systemic Inequality

It takes a comprehensive approach to address systemic inequalities.

Among the crucial tactics are:

Reforming Policy:

Anti-Discrimination Laws: Enacting and enforcing strong anti-discrimination laws can help to prevent discrimination in employment, housing, education, and other areas. *Affirmative Action:* Implementing affirmative action policies can help to level the playing field for marginalized groups.

Progressive Taxation: By taxing higher earners at a higher rate, progressive taxation can aid in the reduction of income inequality.

Social Safety Nets: Vulnerable populations can be protected by robust social safety nets, such as welfare programs and unemployment insurance.

Awareness and Education:

Critical Thinking and Media Literacy: Fighting systemic inequality can be aided by teaching people how to evaluate information critically and confront prejudices.

Training on Diversity and Inclusion: Educating people about diversity, equity, and inclusion can lessen prejudice and discrimination.

Advocacy and Community Organizing:

Activating communities to demand change and support policies that address systemic inequalities is possible through grassroots activism.

Community-Based Organizations: Underserved communities can receive resources and assistance from community-based organizations.

Making Decisions Based on Data:

Data Collection and Analysis: Systemic inequalities can be found and addressed with the aid of data collection and analysis on disparities.

Policies Based on Evidence: More equitable and successful results can result from using data to guide policy decisions.

The intersectional approach

Handling Various Types of Discrimination: Recognizing that individuals may experience multiple forms of discrimination, such as racism, sexism, and classism, is essential for effective interventions.

Opportunities and Difficulties

Addressing systemic inequality is a complex and ongoing challenge.

Some of the challenges include:

Resistance to Change: Powerful individuals and institutions may resist efforts to address systemic inequality.

Lack of Political Will: Instead of tackling systemic inequality, political leaders may give priority to other matters.

Measuring Progress: Since changes may take time to manifest, it can be challenging to gauge how far systemic inequality has been addressed. There are plenty of chances to build a society that is more just and equal in spite of these obstacles. Together, people, groups, and governments can eliminate structural obstacles and create a more welcoming future.

10.2 Encouraging Inclusion and Diversity

A just, equitable, and prosperous society must be built on diversity and inclusion. They entail acknowledging, honoring, and appreciating variations in age, ability, gender, sexual orientation, religion, race, ethnicity, and other traits. Organizations and communities can improve decision-making, stimulate innovation, and improve general well-being by fostering diversity and inclusion.

The Value of Inclusion and Diversity

Enhanced Creativity and Innovation: Diverse teams generate more inventive and creative solutions because they bring a variety of viewpoints, experiences, and ideas to the table.

Better Decision-Making: Diverse teams are better able to solve complex problems and make well-informed decisions.

Improved Reputation: Businesses that put diversity and inclusion first are frequently viewed as more appealing to investors, consumers, and staff.

Greater Job Satisfaction and Employee Morale: An inclusive and diverse workplace can increase job satisfaction and employee morale.

Social Justice: Addressing systemic injustices and advancing social justice are aided by encouraging diversity and inclusion.

Techniques for Fostering Leadership Commitment to Diversity and Inclusion:

Executive Sponsorship: Encouraging diversity and inclusion initiatives requires a strong commitment from the leadership.

Clear Vision and Objectives: Creating specific objectives and plans for diversity and inclusion.

Accountability: Making leaders accountable for accomplishing objectives related to diversity and inclusion.

Hiring and Recruiting:

Diverse Talent Pools: Increasing hiring activities to draw in a varied applicant pool.

Bias-Free Hiring Procedures: Putting in place procedures that are free from bias, like structured interviews and blind resume reviews.

Mentorship and Sponsorship Programs: Giving underrepresented groups access to mentorship and sponsorship opportunities.

An inclusive culture at work:

Open Communication: Promoting candid and open dialogue among staff members.

Respectful Workplace: Establishing an inclusive and courteous workplace.

Offering flexible work schedules in order to meet the needs and preferences of a wide range of people.

Employee Resource Groups (ERGs): ERGs are created to give employees from underrepresented groups networking opportunities and support.

Education and Training:

Inclusion and Diversity Training: Giving staff members instruction on cultural competency, diversity, inclusion, and unconscious bias.
Programs for Leadership Development: cultivating leaders dedicated to inclusivity and diversity.

Data-Based Method:

Monitoring Inclusion and Diversity Metrics: gathering information on metrics related to diversity and inclusion, like employee satisfaction and representation.
Data Analysis: Data analysis is used to determine areas that require improvement and to gauge the success of diversity and inclusion programs.

Overcoming Obstacles

Organizations may encounter difficulties putting effective strategies into practice, even with the advantages of diversity and inclusion.

Opposition to Change: Attempts to advance diversity and inclusion may encounter opposition from certain individuals.

Lack of Knowledge: Advancement may be impeded by a lack of knowledge regarding the significance of diversity and inclusion.

Unconscious Bias: Unconscious biases may affect performance reviews, hiring decisions, and promotions.

Measuring Success: Assessing the results of diversity and inclusion programs can be difficult.

Organizations should place a high priority on training, education, and open communication in order to overcome these obstacles. Organizations can establish a more equitable and effective work environment by cultivating an inclusive and respectful culture.

Encouraging diversity and inclusion is crucial to building a society that is more inventive, just, and equal. Organizations can benefit from having a diverse and inclusive workforce by putting effective strategies into place and resolving issues.

10.3 Creating Communities That Are Robust and Resilient

In order to promote social cohesiveness, economic prosperity, and environmental sustainability, communities must be strong and resilient. Strong social ties, a sense of belonging, and shared values define them. Creating and sustaining such communities calls for a multipronged strategy involving people, groups, and governments.

Important Components of Robust and Resilient Communities

Social Cohesion: Building resilient communities requires strong social ties and a sense of community.

Economic Opportunity: The well-being of individuals and communities depends on having access to jobs, education, and other economic opportunities.

Environmental Sustainability: Long-term community health is influenced by sustainable practices like conservation and renewable energy.

Infrastructure: Community development depends on having enough public services, housing, and transportation infrastructure.

Leadership and Governance: To meet the needs of the community and make wise decisions, effective leadership and governance are essential.

Techniques for Creating Communities That Are Robust and Resilient

Participation and Engagement in the Community:

Forums and Community Meetings: Setting up frequent forums and community meetings to talk about regional issues and concerns.
Civic engagement and voluntarism: motivating locals to donate their time and expertise to nonprofit organizations.
Community-Based Organizations: Assisting local organizations that strive to meet needs in the community.

Inclusion and Social Cohesion:

Intergenerational Programs: Developing initiatives that unite individuals of various ages in order to foster connections and exchange knowledge.
Cultural Diversity and Inclusion: Celebrating cultural differences and advancing diversity and inclusion.

Conflict resolution is the process of creating plans to settle disputes amicably and advance mutual understanding.

Development of the Economy:

Job Creation: Creating jobs by assisting existing companies and luring in new ones.
Entrepreneurship: Supporting small businesses and promoting entrepreneurship.
Putting money into education and training to give people the tools they need to be successful in the workforce is known as skills development.

Sustainability of the Environment:

Green infrastructure: Putting money into parks and other green areas to enhance air quality and lessen flooding.
Sustainable Practices: Encouraging the use of renewable energy sources, waste reduction, and energy conservation.

Getting ready for the effects of climate change, like severe weather and increasing sea levels, is known as climate change adaptation.

Good Governance:

Ensuring that public servants are answerable to the people and behave in the community's best interests is known as transparent and accountable leadership.
Promoting public involvement in decision-making processes is known as citizen participation.
Effective Public Services: Delivering top-notch public services, including public safety, healthcare, and education.

Opportunities and Difficulties

The process of creating communities that are resilient and strong is difficult and fraught with difficulties.

These consist of:

Economic Inequality: Conflict and social division can result from economic inequality.

Social Disintegration: Communities may become weaker when social ties break down.

Environmental Degradation: Communities' health and well-being may be at risk due to environmental degradation.

Political division: Political division can erode social harmony and make resolving issues in the community more challenging.

But there are also plenty of chances to create communities that are more resilient and strong. We can build prosperous, just, and sustainable communities by addressing climate change, advancing social justice, and making educational investments.

Chapter 11:

The Function of Civil Society and Government

In order to shape societies and propel advancement, the government and civil society are essential. Together, they tackle societal issues, advance social justice, and protect citizens' welfare. Although governments have the authority to make laws and carry out policies, civil society organizations serve as an essential check on these powers by standing up for citizens' rights and holding governments responsible.

The Function of the State

Governments are in charge of delivering basic public services like infrastructure, healthcare, and education. They are also essential for maintaining social justice, safeguarding the environment, and controlling the economy.

Important Functions of the Government:

Law and order: upholding the rule of law and preserving public order.

Economic development is the process of fostering economic expansion by means of laws that encourage investment and the creation of jobs.

Social welfare is the provision of safety nets for vulnerable groups, such as welfare programs and unemployment insurance.

Infrastructure development is the process of spending money on things like public transportation, roads, and bridges in order to boost the economy and enhance people's quality of life.

Environmental Protection: Protecting the environment by putting environmental laws and policies into effect.

International relations: Practicing diplomacy and representing the country abroad.

Civil Society's Function

Non-governmental organizations (NGOs), community groups, and social movements are examples of civil society organizations that are essential in promoting social change, offering assistance, and holding governments responsible.

Crucial Functions of Civil Society:

Advocacy: Promoting environmental preservation, human rights, and social justice.

Service delivery is the provision of basic services, especially in places where government services are insufficient, such as healthcare, education, and social welfare.

Accountability and Monitoring: keeping an eye on government activities and making them answerable for their policies and procedures.

Community development is the process of giving local communities the tools they need to overcome obstacles and enhance their standard of living.

Creating novel answers to societal issues is known as social innovation.

The Interaction Between Civil Society and Government

In order to solve social problems and advance the general welfare, the government and civil society frequently collaborate.

This partnership can take many different forms:

Policy Advocacy: By promoting particular laws or rules, civil society organizations can have an impact on governmental policy.

Partnerships for Service Delivery: To provide public services like healthcare and education, governments and non-governmental organizations can collaborate.

Public service co-production: Civil society organizations and governments can collaborate to co-produce public services, like community development programs.

Social Accountability: Civil society groups have the ability to keep an eye on how well the government is performing and holding representatives responsible for their deeds.

Opportunities and Difficulties

Civil society and the government both have important roles to play in forming society, but they also face difficulties.

These consist of:

Corruption and Inefficiency: These two issues have the potential to reduce the efficacy of civil society organizations and the government.

Political Polarization: Government and civil society cooperation may be hampered by political polarization.

Resource Limitations: The capacity of governments and civil society organizations to tackle social and environmental issues may be restricted by resource limitations.

Notwithstanding these obstacles, there are plenty of chances for civil society and the government to collaborate in order to build more sustainable, just, and equitable future. We can address the complex issues facing our world by leveraging technology, building strong partnerships, and encouraging accountability and transparency.

11.1 The Importance of Efficient Governance

For societies to thrive and for countries to develop sustainably, effective governance is crucial. It includes the procedures of accountability, decision-making, and the use of political power to run a nation's affairs. All citizens' needs are satisfied, resources are used effectively, and public institutions are open and accountable when there is good governance in place.

Essential Elements of Successful Governance

Participation: People ought to be able to take part in the decisions that impact their daily lives.

Rule of law: Rules ought to be transparent, equitable, and applied uniformly to everyone.

Accountability and Transparency: Public servants should be held responsible for their choices, and government actions should be transparent.

Governments ought to be receptive to the wants and needs of their constituents.

Equity and Inclusivity: It is the responsibility of governments to guarantee that all citizens receive fair treatment and equal opportunities.

Effectiveness and Efficiency: Governments should use public resources and provide public services in an efficient manner.

Obstacles to Efficient Governance

Even though effective governance is crucial, many nations struggle to put good governance principles into practice.

Among the main difficulties are:

Corruption: Corruption can impede economic growth and compromise the efficiency of government institutions.

Political Uncertainty: Political unpredictability can impede long-term planning and cause uncertainty.

Inequality: Social and economic disparities can erode governmental legitimacy and lead to social unrest.

Weak Institutions: The application of good governance may be impeded by weak institutions, such as the legislature and the judiciary.

Absence of Accountability and Transparency: These two factors can result in the abuse of authority and the misappropriation of public funds.

The Value of Effective Governance

There are various reasons why good governance is crucial.

Economic Growth: By encouraging trade, investment, and innovation, good governance can foster an atmosphere that is favorable to economic growth.

Social Development: Poverty reduction, health improvement, and educational improvement are all aided by good governance.

Environmental Protection: Sustainable development and environmental protection are two benefits of effective governance.

Political Stability: Peace and conflict avoidance can be facilitated by effective governance.

Human Rights: Social justice and human rights can be safeguarded by efficient governance.

Techniques to Enhance Governance

There are several actions that citizens and governments can take to enhance governance:

Investing in government institutions' ability to provide efficient public services is known as ***"institutional strengthening."***

Encouraging Transparency and Accountability: Putting policies in place to promote transparency and accountability, like independent audits and laws pertaining to freedom of information.

Promoting Citizen Participation: Giving people the ability to take part in decision-making procedures through public consultations, elections, and other means.

Combating Corruption: Putting anti-corruption strategies into action, like bolstering law enforcement and encouraging moral conduct.

Encouraging International Cooperation: International collaboration can support the advancement of good governance standards and norms.

Governments can enhance governance and build a better future for their citizens by tackling these issues and putting effective plans into place.

11.2 The importance of citizen engagement

A fundamental component of democracies is citizen participation. Voting, volunteering, protesting, and pushing for change are all examples of citizens' active engagement in public life. Citizens can impact decision-making, hold leaders responsible, and mold the future of their society by actively participating in their communities and governments.

The Significance of Citizen Engagement

Strengthening Democracy: A robust democracy depends on citizen participation. It guarantees that the government responds to the people's wants and needs.

Enhancing Governance: By encouraging transparency and holding public officials accountable, active citizen participation can aid in enhancing the quality of governance.

Encouraging Social Justice: Addressing social and economic disparities and advancing social justice can be accomplished through citizen engagement.

Improving Community Development: By volunteering, taking part in neighborhood projects, and pushing for reform, involved citizens can support the growth of their communities.

Promoting Civic Virtue: A sense of civic obligation and responsibility can be fostered through citizen engagement.

Types of Participation by Citizens

There are numerous ways to engage citizens, including:

Voting: Citizens have a fundamental right and obligation to cast ballots in elections.

Volunteering: Contributing to charities and community organizations can help to foster a sense of community and address social needs.

Advocacy: Promoting particular causes, like social justice, human rights, or climate change, can have an impact on public policy and societal transformation.

Giving: Contributions to nonprofit organizations can help solve social issues and promote worthy causes.

Protesting: Nonviolent demonstrations can be an effective means of voicing disapproval and calling for reform.

Using social media to advocate for social change, rally support, and increase awareness is known as social media activism.

Running for Office: One direct way to have an impact on governmental policy and decision-making is to run for public office.

Obstacles to Involving Citizens

Despite its significance, there are a number of obstacles to citizen engagement:

Cynicism and Apathy: Cynicism and apathy can deter people from getting involved in public life. Absence of knowledge and instruction People's capacity to participate may be restricted by a lack of knowledge and instruction regarding civic engagement.

Participation Barriers: People's capacity to engage in elections and other political processes may be restricted by systemic obstacles like gerrymandering and voter suppression.

Time Restrictions: People may find it challenging to engage in civic activities due to hectic schedules and other obligations.

Promoting Involvement of Citizens

In order to promote increased citizen participation, it is crucial to:

Encourage Civic Education: Teaching young people about their civic rights, obligations, and the democratic process can motivate them to take an active role in society.

Empower Communities: Giving communities the tools they need to take charge of neighborhood problems can promote a feeling of pride and community.

Simplify the Voting Process: Voter turnout can be raised by making it simpler to register to vote and cast a ballot.

Encourage Volunteerism: Encouraging people to volunteer and providing them with chances to give back to their communities.

Use Technology: Making use of technological tools, such as social media campaigns, online petitions, and e-government platforms, to promote civic engagement.

Establishing a culture that values civic engagement and motivates individuals to become active in their communities is known as ***"fostering a culture of civic engagement."***
We can create societies that are more robust, resilient, and democratic by encouraging citizen participation.

11.3 The role of international organizations

To address global issues and advance international cooperation, international organizations are essential. These groups, which are made up of independent states, cooperate to accomplish shared objectives like preserving peace and security, advancing economic growth, and defending human rights.

Important Functions of International Organizations in Preserving World Peace and Security:

United Nations (UN): The main international body in charge of preserving world peace and security is the UN. It seeks to uphold human rights, mediate conflicts, and avert conflicts.

Regional Organizations: Key roles in regional security and cooperation are played by regional organizations such as the Association of Southeast Asian Nations (ASEAN), the African Union (AU), and the European Union (EU).

Encouraging Economic Collaboration:

International Monetary Fund (IMF): The IMF seeks to foster economic expansion and stabilize the world economy.

World Bank: To combat poverty and advance sustainable development, the World Bank offers developing nations financial and technical support.

World Trade Organization (WTO): The WTO helps settle trade disputes and regulates international trade laws.

Taking on Global Challenges:

Climate Change: To combat climate change and advance sustainable development, organizations such as the United Nations Framework Convention on Climate Change (UNFCCC) are in operation.

Public Health: The World Health Organization (WHO) is in charge of international initiatives to enhance public health and address medical emergencies.

Human Rights: Human rights are promoted and safeguarded globally by institutions such as the United Nations Human Rights Council.

Giving Aid to Humanitarians:

UNHCR, or the United Nations High Commissioner for Refugees: Internally displaced people and refugees are protected and assisted by the UNHCR.

WFP, or the World Food Programme: Millions of individuals who suffer from hunger and food insecurity receive food assistance from the WFP.

Obstacles and Restrictions

International organizations are essential in tackling global issues, but they also confront a number of difficulties:

Sovereignty: It can be challenging to strike a balance between international cooperation and national sovereignty.

Political Differences: Effective cooperation may be hampered by disparate national interests and political philosophies.

Resource Limitations: International organizations may experience resource limitations that restrict their capacity to carry out initiatives and accomplish their objectives.

Bureaucracy: International organizations' ability to make decisions quickly and effectively can be hampered by bureaucratic procedures.

Enforcement Mechanisms: To guarantee that their decisions are followed, international organizations frequently lack efficient enforcement mechanisms.

The Prospects for Global Collaboration

International cooperation is still necessary to address global issues in spite of these obstacles.

There are various actions that can be taken to improve international cooperation:

Investing in and equipping international organizations to handle global issues is known as ***"strengthening international institutions."***
Encouraging multilateral cooperation to tackle intricate global issues is known as ***"promoting multilateralism."***
Encouraging Communication and Diplomacy: Encouraging communication and diplomacy to settle conflicts amicably.
Supporting Civil Society: Giving civil society groups the tools they need to fight for human rights and international justice.

Changing with the World: International organizations need to be able to adjust to the evolving global environment, which includes changes in geopolitics and technology.

Together, nations can overcome obstacles, advance prosperity and peace, and build a brighter future for everybody.

Part IV:

A Vision for the Future

Chapter 12:

Emerging Technologies and Their Impact

Globally, industries, economies, and societies are changing as a result of the quick development of technology. New technologies are changing how we live and work, spurring innovation, and increasing productivity. But there are drawbacks and moral dilemmas to these technological developments as well.

Important New Technologies: AI (Artificial Intelligence)

Algorithms that let computers learn from data without explicit programming are known as machine learning algorithms.

The ability of computers to comprehend and process human language is known as natural language processing, or NLP.

The ability of computers to decipher and comprehend visual data from their environment is known as computer vision.

IoT, or the Internet of Things, is the ability of devices to gather and share data due to their interconnection.

Blockchain Technology: a safe, decentralized digital ledger that keeps track of transactions on several computers.

Biotechnology: using biological processes to create new products and technologies.

Robotics: the planning, building, and use of robots.

Effects on the Community

Society is being significantly impacted by these new technologies:

Economic Growth: By generating new sectors, occupations, and business models, technological developments can stimulate economic growth.

Better Healthcare: By facilitating drug discovery, personalized medicine, and early disease detection, artificial intelligence (AI) and biotechnology has the potential to completely transform healthcare.

Improved Education: By personalizing learning experiences, technology can increase the effectiveness and accessibility of education.

Enhanced Productivity: AI and automation have the potential to boost efficiency and productivity across a range of sectors.

Social Change: By fostering connections, empowering underrepresented groups, and advancing social justice, technology can help bring about social change.

Difficulties and Moral Aspects

Although new technologies have a lot of promise, there are drawbacks and moral dilemmas as well.

Job displacement: Workers may need to adjust to new roles and skills as a result of automation and artificial intelligence.

Privacy Issues: Data security and privacy are issues brought up by the massive volumes of data being collected and analyzed.

__Implications for Ethics:__ The creation and application of artificial intelligence (AI) and other cutting-edge technologies bring up moral issues, including the possibility of prejudice and discrimination.

__Digital Divide:__ Social and economic disparities can be made worse by unequal access to technology.

Technology's Future

As technology advances, it is critical to think about how it might affect society and to create moral standards and laws.

Among the upcoming trends are:

__Hyperautomation:__ The automation of tasks and procedures across industries through the use of cutting-edge technologies.

Virtual reality and augmented reality are immersive technologies that can improve work, play, and education.

Strong computers that can resolve complicated issues far more quickly than traditional computers are known as quantum computers.

Biotechnology and Gene Editing: Biotechnology breakthroughs like CRISPR have the potential to completely transform both agriculture and medicine.

Investing in R&D, fostering digital literacy, and addressing ethical issues are essential to achieving the full potential of emerging technologies. Governments, corporations, and individuals can all benefit from collaborating to shape the direction of technology.

12.1 Artificial Intelligence: Two-Sided Weapon

One of the most revolutionary technologies of our time is artificial intelligence (AI), which has the power to completely alter both industries and societies. But great power also comes with great responsibility, and AI has serious risks that should be carefully evaluated.

AI's Promise

AI has the potential to help billions of people live better lives and solve some of the most important problems facing the planet.

Among the possible advantages of AI are:

Healthcare: AI has the potential to transform healthcare by facilitating more precise diagnosis, earlier disease detection, and individualized treatment regimens.

Education: By personalizing learning experiences, AI-powered tools can increase the effectiveness and accessibility of education.

Transportation: Autonomous vehicles, such as self-driving cars, can increase the efficiency and safety of transportation.

Climate Change: AI can be used to create novel responses to climate change, like predicting natural disasters and optimizing energy use.

Economic Growth: By automating processes, increasing productivity, and spawning new industries, AI can stimulate economic growth.

AI's Dangers

Although AI has many advantages, there are also possible risks:

Job displacement: As AI develops, it may result in the loss of jobs across a range of industries.

Bias and Discrimination: If AI systems are trained on biased data, they may reinforce prejudice and discrimination.

Privacy Issues: Data security and privacy are issues brought up by the massive volumes of data being collected and analyzed.

Autonomous Weapons: Because of the possibility of unforeseen consequences, the development of autonomous weapons systems presents ethical questions.

Existential Risk: According to some experts, if advanced AI gets out of control, it could endanger humankind.

Reducing the Hazards

It is crucial to create and put into effect ethical standards and laws in order to reduce the risks associated with AI.

Among the important factors are:

Transparency: In order for users to comprehend how decisions are made, AI systems should be clear and explicable.

Fairness: AI systems ought to be impartial and equitable by design.

Accountability: The creation and application of AI systems should be the responsibility of both individuals and organizations.

Safety: AI systems ought to be developed and examined to make sure they are dependable and safe.

International Cooperation: To handle the global opportunities and challenges presented by AI, international cooperation is crucial.

AI's Future

Although AI's future is unclear, it will undoubtedly have a significant impact on our daily lives. By carefully weighing the possible advantages and disadvantages, we can use AI to improve everyone's future.

Promoting ethical development and deployment, making investments in education and training, and fostering international cooperation are all essential to ensuring that AI is used for good. We can influence AI's future for the betterment of humanity if we band together.

12.2 Biotechnology and its implications for healthcare and agriculture

Biotechnology: A Two-Sided Blade

The use of biological processes to create products and services, or biotechnology, has transformed many sectors, most notably agriculture and healthcare. Some of the most important issues facing the world today, like hunger, disease, and environmental degradation, may be resolved by it. But it also brings up possible dangers and ethical issues.

Healthcare Biotechnology

Because it has made it possible to create novel treatments and therapies, biotechnology has greatly improved healthcare.

Genetic engineering: Researchers can create novel medications, vaccines, and treatments by changing an organism's genetic composition. For instance, genetically modified organisms *(GMOs)* can be used to increase crop yields and gene therapy can be used to treat genetic diseases.

Biopharmaceuticals: The creation of biopharmaceuticals—drugs made with living organisms—is a result of biotechnology. Numerous illnesses, such as diabetes, autoimmune disorders, and cancer, can be treated with these medications.

Diagnostic Tools: The development of sensitive and specific diagnostic tests, like PCR and ELISA, made possible by biotechnology can aid in the early and precise diagnosis of diseases.

The goal of regenerative medicine is to use stem cells and other biological methods to restore damaged tissues and organs.

Agricultural Biotechnology

Agriculture has also changed as a result of biotechnology, with higher crop yields, better nutritional value, and increased disease and pest resistance.

Genetic Modification: Through genetic modification, crops can acquire desired characteristics like enhanced nutritional value, higher yield, and resistance to pests and herbicides.

Beneficial microorganisms found in biofertilizers can increase soil fertility and lessen the need for chemical fertilizers.

Biopesticides: Made from natural sources, biopesticides can be used to manage diseases and pests without causing environmental harm.

Potential Hazards and Ethical Issues

Biotechnology has a lot of promise, but it also presents risks and ethical questions.

Impact on the Environment: The introduction of genetically modified organisms into the environment may result in unforeseen outcomes, like the emergence of weeds that are resistant to herbicides.

Social and Economic Inequality: Social and economic inequality may be exacerbated by unequal access to biotechnology and its products.

Ethical Concerns: Genetic engineering and the use of biotechnology in human reproduction present moral dilemmas regarding the modification of human life.

Biosafety and Biosecurity: When biotechnology is misused, it can lead to major issues like the development of biological weapons.

Biotechnology's Future

Biotechnology has a bright future because it can help solve many of the most important problems facing the globe. However, in order to guarantee the responsible use of biotechnology, ethical guidelines and regulations must be developed and put into effect.

We can use biotechnology to enhance human health, safeguard the environment, and build a sustainable future by carefully weighing the possible advantages and disadvantages.

12.3 Nanotechnology and its applications in various fields

Nanotechnology: An Entire Universe of Miniature Wonders

The manipulation of matter at the atomic and molecular level, or nanotechnology, is transforming a wide range of disciplines, including materials science and medicine. This new technology has enormous potential to solve world problems and raise living standards.

Nanotechnology: What is it?

Working with particles ranging in size from 1 to 100 nanometers is a part of nanotechnology. Materials display special qualities at this scale that can be used for a variety of purposes.

Nanotechnology Applications: Medicine

Drug Delivery: By delivering medications straight to target cells, nanomaterials can increase effectiveness and lessen side effects.

Medical Imaging: Contrast agents based on nanotechnology can improve the resolution of CT and MRI scans, among other medical imaging procedures.

Tissue Engineering: Scaffolds for organ engineering and tissue regeneration can be made with nanomaterials.

Biosensors: Nanosensors are able to track health conditions in real time and identify diseases in their early stages.

Science of Materials

Stronger and Lighter Materials: Materials that are stronger, lighter, and more resilient can be made using nanomaterials.

Surfaces that clean themselves: Nanomaterials can produce surfaces that are impervious to water and dirt.

Energy Storage: Batteries and other energy storage devices can have their capacity and efficiency increased by using nanomaterials.

Electronic devices

Faster and Smaller Electronics: Electronic devices that are faster and smaller can be made using nanomaterials.

Flexible Electronics: Wearable and flexible electronics are made possible by nanotechnology.

Quantum Computing: Quantum computers, which have the potential to completely transform computing power, can be created using nanomaterials.

Science of the Environment

Water Purification: Impurities can be eliminated from water by filtering it with nanomaterials.

Pollution Control: Advanced materials for reducing air and water pollution can be created using nanotechnology.

Sustainable Energy: Solar cells and other renewable energy technologies can operate more efficiently thanks to nanomaterials.

Obstacles and Things to Think About

Although nanotechnology has a lot of promise, there are drawbacks and moral dilemmas as well.

Health and Environmental Risks: It is important to carefully evaluate the possible health and environmental risks associated with nanomaterials.

Implications for Ethics: Nanotechnology's ethical ramifications need to be carefully considered, especially in fields like genetic engineering and human enhancement.

Regulatory Framework: It is crucial to create efficient regulations to control the advancement and application of nanotechnology.

Accessibility and Cost: Access to nanotechnology may be restricted by the high expense of research and development, especially in developing nations.

Nanotechnology's Future

Nanotechnology has a promising future and has the power to completely transform a lot of facets of our lives. But it's crucial to use this technology carefully and make sure it's applied morally and sensibly. We can use nanotechnology to improve everyone's future by resolving the issues and optimizing the advantages.

Chapter 13:

A Sustainable Future: Juggling Development with the Environment

The global challenge of sustainable development necessitates a comprehensive strategy to strike a balance between environmental preservation, social justice, and economic growth. It entails making decisions that satisfy current demands without endangering the capacity of future generations to satisfy their own.

The Foundations of Sustainability

The foundation of sustainable development is threefold:

Economic Sustainability: The goal of this pillar is to guarantee sustained economic expansion and advancement. It includes tactics like fair trade, sustainable business practices, and equitable wealth distribution.

Social Sustainability: This pillar places a strong emphasis on social justice, human rights, and equity. It entails dealing with problems like social exclusion, poverty, and inequality.

Environmental Sustainability: The preservation of the environment and natural resources is the main goal of this pillar. It entails lowering pollution, preserving energy, and slowing down global warming.

Obstacles to Sustainable Development

A number of obstacles stand in the way of achieving sustainable development:

Climate Change: The environment, economies, and societies around the world are all seriously threatened by climate change.

Resource Depletion: Scarcity and environmental damage can result from overuse of natural resources, such as water and minerals.

Pollution: The environment and human health can be negatively impacted by pollution originating from a variety of sources, such as transportation and industrial operations.

Poverty and Inequality: These two issues can worsen social and environmental issues and obstruct efforts at sustainable development.

Political Instability: Attempts to attain sustainable development may be hampered by political instability.

Techniques for a Sustainable Future

We must take a multifaceted approach that includes the following in order to achieve a sustainable future:

International Cooperation: To address global issues like poverty and climate change, international cooperation is crucial.

Sustainable Production and Consumption: It is essential to promote sustainable consumption habits, such as recycling, cutting waste, and selecting sustainable goods.

Greenhouse gas emissions can be decreased by switching to renewable energy sources like solar, wind, and hydropower.

Sustainable Agriculture: Using sustainable farming methods, like agroforestry and organic farming, can help preserve the environment and guarantee food security.

Green Infrastructure: Putting money into green spaces like parks and green roofs can help to make communities healthier, lower flooding, and improve air quality.

Education and Awareness: Giving people knowledge about environmental issues and sustainability can enable them to make wise decisions.

Policy and Regulation: To safeguard the environment and advance sustainable development, strict environmental laws and policies are required.

Technology and Innovation: Research and development expenditures can result in creative answers to societal and environmental problems.

Individuals' Role

Making thoughtful decisions in their daily lives is another way that individuals can support sustainable development.

Here are a few easy steps:

Minimizing waste and conserving resources through the reduction, reuse, and recycling of materials.

Water and energy conservation: shutting off water and lights when not in use.

Selecting Sustainable Products: Purchasing goods made in an ethical and ecologically responsible manner.

Helping Sustainable Businesses: Assisting companies that put sustainability first.

Promoting Change: Pushing for laws that support environmental preservation and sustainability.

Governments, corporations, and individuals can all work together to build a more sustainable future for future generations.

13.1 Renewable Energy and the Low-Carbon Economy

Addressing climate change and securing a sustainable future require a global shift to a low-carbon economy. In this shift, renewable energy sources like solar, wind, hydro, and geothermal power are essential. We can lessen the effects of climate change and create a more resilient planet by encouraging clean energy and cutting greenhouse gas emissions.

Being Aware of the Low-Carbon Economy

An economic system that seeks to minimize its impact on the environment and cut down on greenhouse gas emissions is known as a low-carbon economy. It entails switching to cleaner, renewable energy sources from fossil fuels.

A low-carbon economy's salient characteristics include:

Energy Efficiency: Increasing building, transportation, and industrial energy efficiency. Increasing the use of renewable energy sources, such as geothermal, hydro, wind, and solar power.

Sustainable Transportation: Encouraging environmentally friendly modes of transportation like public transportation and electric cars.

Recycling, reusing, and remanufacturing are ways to reduce waste and conserve resources in the circular economy.

The process of capturing and storing carbon dioxide emissions from power plants and industrial facilities is known as carbon capture and storage, or CCS.

Renewable Energy's Function

Fossil fuels can be replaced with clean, sustainable energy from renewable sources. They could lessen the effects of climate change and drastically cut greenhouse gas emissions.

Solar Energy: Using photovoltaic cells to capture solar energy.

Wind Energy: Using wind turbines to transform wind energy into electrical power.

Using the kinetic energy of flowing water to generate electricity is known as hydropower.

Geothermal energy is the process of producing electricity by harnessing the heat that exists within the Earth.

Making energy from biomass, such as wood and agricultural waste, is known as bioenergy.

Opportunities and Difficulties

There are various obstacles in the way of the shift to a low-carbon economy:

Initial Investment Costs: Renewable energy technologies may come with hefty upfront costs.

Renewable Energy Source Intermittency: Energy storage solutions are necessary due to the intermittent nature of renewable energy sources, such as solar and wind power.

Frameworks for Policies and Regulations: To encourage investment in clean energy and deter carbon-intensive activities, effective policies and regulations are required.

Public Perception and Acceptance: The effective implementation of renewable energy projects depends on public acceptance and support.

The shift to a low-carbon economy offers substantial opportunities in spite of these obstacles:

Employment Creation: Manufacturing, installation, and maintenance jobs may be generated by the renewable energy industry.

Economic Growth: Innovation and economic growth can be stimulated by investments in clean technologies.

Better Air Quality: Public health and air quality can be enhanced by reducing dependency on fossil fuels.

Climate Change Mitigation: Reducing the effects of climate change requires a shift to a low-carbon economy.

Energy's Future

Traditional and renewable energy sources will probably coexist in the energy landscape of the future. Renewable energy is predicted to become more and more significant in the world's energy mix as costs continue to drop and technology develops. We can build a more resilient and sustainable future for future generations by adopting a low-carbon economy and making investments in renewable energy.

13.2 Urban Planning and Sustainable Cities

Cities that put an emphasis on social, economic, and environmental sustainability are known as sustainable cities. Their goal is to build resilient, equitable, and livable communities while reducing their environmental impact. By taking into account elements like community development, infrastructure, transportation, and land use, urban planning is essential to creating sustainable cities.

Promoting dense, mixed-use development to lessen urban sprawl and increase walkability is one of the main tenets of sustainable urban planning and compact development.

Sustainable Transportation: To lessen dependency on automobiles and enhance air quality, public transportation, cycling, and walking should be prioritized.

Green infrastructure is the process of incorporating green areas, like parks and green roofs, into cities to enhance biodiversity, reduce flooding, and improve air quality.

Energy Efficiency: To cut greenhouse gas emissions, energy-efficient infrastructure and buildings should be promoted.

Waste Reduction and Recycling: To reduce the impact on the environment, waste reduction and recycling programs should be put into place.

Water conservation: preserving water through creative technology and effective use.

Social equity is the guarantee that every citizen has access to basic services, reasonably priced housing, and chances for both social and economic growth.

Opportunities and Difficulties

Although there are many advantages to sustainable urban planning, there are also many obstacles to overcome:

Rapid Urbanization: Infrastructure and resources may be strained by rapid urbanization.

Climate Change: Urban problems like flooding and heat islands may get worse due to climate change.

Inequality: Social and economic inequality can be very prevalent in urban areas.

Infrastructure Investment: Putting money into environmentally friendly infrastructure can be expensive.

Notwithstanding these obstacles, there are numerous advantages to sustainable urban planning:

Better Quality of Life: With clean air, green areas, and less traffic, sustainable cities can provide a better quality of life.

Economic Growth: Job creation and investment are two benefits of sustainable cities.

Decreased Environmental Impact: Climate change can be lessened and the environment can be protected with the aid of sustainable urban planning.

Social Cohesion: Cities with sound planning can promote community involvement and social cohesion.

Examples of Sustainable Urban Cases

Globally, a number of cities have become shining examples of sustainable urban development:

Copenhagen, Denmark: renowned for its dedication to sustainability, clean energy projects, and bike-friendly infrastructure.

Portland, Oregon: A leader in sustainable urban planning, emphasizing green building, urban agriculture, and transit-oriented development.

Singapore: A city-state that has made significant investments in green areas, renewable energy, and sustainable infrastructure.

Colombia's Medellin is a city that has changed through creative urban design, social services, and public transit.

Sustainable Cities' Future

Sustainable cities of the future will require ongoing adaptation and innovation. New technologies, like smart city technologies, can improve transportation, maximize resource use, and improve urban dwellers' quality of life. Furthermore, the shift to sustainable urban development can be accelerated through global collaboration and knowledge exchange.

We can build resilient, just, and ecologically friendly cities by adopting sustainable urban planning concepts. In addition to helping the present generation, this will guarantee a sustainable future for future generations.

13.3 Preservation and Preservation of Biodiversity

The variety of life on Earth, or biodiversity, is vital to both the health of our planet and human well-being. However, biodiversity is being threatened at an alarming rate by human activities like pollution, deforestation, and climate change. To preserve the natural heritage of our planet and guarantee a sustainable future, conservation and biodiversity protection are essential.

The Significance of Biodiversity

In order to sustain life and keep ecosystems in balance, biodiversity is essential.

Among the main advantages of biodiversity are:

Ecosystem Services: Pollination, water purification, and climate regulation are just a few of the vital ecosystem services that biodiversity offers.

Food Security: Because biodiversity produces a range of crops and livestock, it is crucial for food security.

Medicinal Resources: Plants and animals are the source of many medications, and biodiversity can lead to the development of novel medications and therapies.

Cultural and Aesthetic Value: By fostering our sense of place, generating artistic and cultural inspiration, and offering recreational opportunities, biodiversity enhances our lives.

Endangering Biodiversity

Various threats endanger biodiversity globally:

Habitat Loss and Fragmentation: Natural habitats are being destroyed by agriculture, urbanization, and deforestation.

Overexploitation: Populations can be weakened by overfishing, overhunting, and overharvesting of resources.

Pollution: Runoff from cities, farms, and industrial processes can damage ecosystems and endanger wildlife.

Climate Change: Temperature, precipitation patterns, and ocean acidity are all changing as a result of climate change.

Invasive species have the potential to upset ecosystems and outcompete native species.

Strategies for Conservation

A range of conservation techniques can be used to preserve biodiversity:

Protected Areas: One way to preserve biodiversity is to create national parks, wildlife sanctuaries, and other protected areas.

Habitat Restoration: Biodiversity can be restored by replanting degraded ecosystems, such as wetlands and forests.

Sustainable Use: The impact on biodiversity can be reduced by encouraging the sustainable use of natural resources, such as sustainable forestry and fisheries.

Implementing conservation initiatives for threatened species, such as reintroduction and captive breeding, is known as species conservation.

International Cooperation: Working together with other nations to combat global biodiversity threats like illegal wildlife trade and climate change.

Community-Based Conservation: Long-term sustainability can be ensured by involving local communities in conservation initiatives.

Individuals' Role

People can also contribute to biodiversity conservation by adopting sustainable lifestyle choices.

Reduce, Reuse, Recycle: Cutting back on waste, recycling materials, and reusing products can all help save resources and lessen pollution.

Conserve Energy and Water: Reducing the impact on the environment can be achieved by conserving energy and water.

Encourage Sustainable Businesses: Businesses can embrace more ecologically friendly practices by selecting sustainable goods and services.

Volunteer for Conservation Organizations: You can contribute to biodiversity conservation by volunteering with conservation organizations.

Inform Others: Informing people about the value of biodiversity and the dangers it faces can spur them to take action.

Governments, groups, and individuals can safeguard biodiversity and guarantee a sustainable future for everybody by cooperating.

Chapter 14:

A World That Is Fairer and More Just

For centuries, people have worked to create a more fair and just world. Everyone has equal opportunities in this world, irrespective of their socioeconomic background, gender, race, ethnicity, or religion. To build a peaceful and successful society, this ideal is necessary.

The Value of Equity and Justice

Social Harmony: By reducing conflict and fostering understanding among various groups, justice and equity help to foster social harmony.

Economic Growth: By guaranteeing that everyone has the chance to contribute to the economy, a just and equitable society can promote economic growth.

Human Flourishing: People can live happy, fulfilling lives and realize their full potential when they are given equal opportunities.

Global Stability: There is a greater chance of stability and peace in a world founded on justice and equity.

Important Obstacles in the Way of Justice and Equity

Even with great advancements, there are still many obstacles in the way of creating a more fair and just society.

Among the main difficulties are:

Systemic Inequality: Injustice is still sustained by ingrained systemic inequalities like racism, sexism, and classism.

Inequality and Poverty: These two issues restrict opportunities and prolong cycles of disadvantage.

Political Polarization: Political polarization can make it challenging to find common ground and impede progress on social justice issues.

Climate Change: The effects of climate change worsen already-existing disparities and disproportionately impact marginalized communities.

Techniques for Creating a More Fair and Just Society

We must take a multifaceted approach that tackles the underlying causes of inequality if we are to build a more just and equitable world.

Among the crucial tactics are:

Education and Awareness: Education is a potent instrument for advancing equity and social justice. We can promote empathy and understanding by teaching people about problems like poverty, racism, and sexism.

Policy Reform: Policies that encourage equality and lessen inequality can be put into place by governments. Affirmative action, social safety nets, and progressive taxes are a few examples of policies that can help level the playing field.

Community Organizing: This strategy can enable underrepresented groups to fight for their rights and interests.

International Cooperation: To address global issues like poverty, climate change, and violations of human rights, international cooperation is crucial.

Individual Actions: By making thoughtful decisions in their day-to-day lives, people can help create a more fair and just society. This includes volunteering, contributing to charitable causes, and endorsing morally upright companies.

An Urgent Appeal

It takes a team effort to create a more fair and just world. Together, we have the power to build a society in which everyone can prosper.

We can begin by:

Educating Ourselves: Acquiring knowledge of social justice concerns and the structural obstacles that sustain inequality.

Taking Action: Giving to charitable causes, volunteering, and taking part in social and political movements.

Speaking out against discrimination and injustice is known as ***"challenging injustice."***

Fostering Understanding and Empathy: Creating connections between individuals from various backgrounds.

Endorsing Equity-Promoting Policies: Promoting laws that deal with structural inequalities.

We can get closer to a society where everyone has the chance to realize their full potential by implementing these actions.

14.1 Social Justice and Human Rights

The pursuit of a just and equitable society is based on the fundamental ideas of social justice and human rights. Human rights and social justice are intertwined, with social justice guaranteeing the realization of human rights and human rights acting as its cornerstone.

Comprehending Social Justice and Human Rights

Human Rights: Regardless of nationality, ethnicity, gender, religion, or any other status, all people are entitled to these fundamental rights. Civil, political, economic, social, and cultural rights are among them.

The freedom of thought, conscience, and religion; the freedom of expression and opinion; the right to life, liberty, and personal security; and the right to take part in the political process are all considered civil and political rights.

International.joshandmak.com
The rights to employment, education, decent housing, healthcare, and social security are all considered economic, social, and cultural rights. A fair distribution of resources, opportunities, and privileges within a community is known as social justice. It entails resolving structural injustices and guaranteeing that every

individual has the opportunity to realize their greatest potential.

The Relationship Between Social Justice and Human Rights

Social justice and human rights are intimately related. Human rights must be realized for social justice to exist, and social justice must exist for human rights to be safeguarded. For instance, although the right to education is a basic human right, it cannot be fully achieved unless structural injustices that restrict access to high-quality education are addressed.

Human Rights and Social Justice Issues

The realization of social justice and human rights is still hampered by a number of issues, despite tremendous advancements in recent decades:

Poverty and Inequality: These two issues can prolong cycles of disadvantage and restrict access to basic services like healthcare and education.

Discrimination: Human rights violations and social injustice may result from discrimination on the basis of race, gender, ethnicity, religion, or other characteristics.

Violence and Conflict: These two factors have the power to uproot populations, demolish infrastructure, and compromise human rights.

Climate Change: Human rights issues may arise as a result of climate change, which may also make already-existing disparities worse.

Rapid technological advancements and ethical concerns: Privacy, surveillance, and the possibility of discrimination are ethical issues brought up by these developments.

Encouraging Social Justice and Human Rights Promoting social justice and human rights requires:

Strengthen International Institutions: Promoting and defending human rights is a major responsibility of international organizations like the United Nations.

Encourage Human Rights Education: Teaching others about human rights can help to create a more respectful and tolerant society.

Encourage Civil Society Organizations: When it comes to promoting social justice and human rights, civil society organizations can be extremely important.

Encourage the Implementation of Just Policies: Governments ought to enact laws that uphold human rights and advance social justice.

Participate in International Cooperation: Addressing global issues and advancing human rights require international cooperation.

Together, we can create a world that is more fair and just and where everyone can realize their full potential.

14.2 International Collaboration and Diplomacy

International cooperation and diplomacy are now vital instruments for tackling global issues in a world that is becoming more interconnected by the day. Countries can solve complicated issues, advance peace and security, and stimulate economic growth by cooperating.

International Cooperation's Significance

There are several reasons why international cooperation is essential.

Taking on Global Challenges: We must work together to address global concerns like poverty, terrorism, and climate change.

Encouraging Peace and Security: International collaboration and diplomacy can aid in averting wars and fostering peace.

Promoting Economic Growth: Foreign investment and trade have the potential to boost employment and economic expansion.

Sharing Technology and Knowledge: To solve global issues, nations can exchange technology and knowledge and learn from one another.

Important Players in International Collaboration IGOs, or intergovernmental organizations: Coordination of global efforts is greatly aided by international organizations like the United Nations, the World Trade Organization, and the International Monetary Fund.

WorldInfoTravel.com

Non-Governmental Organizations (NGOs): NGOs can support social and environmental causes and have an impact on policy decisions.

Multinational Corporations: Although they have a big influence on social issues and the environment, multinational corporations can also help the world economy grow and develop.

Individuals: Through activism, volunteer work, and conscious consumption, individuals can support global cooperation.

Obstacles to Global Collaboration

Despite its significance, there are a number of obstacles to international cooperation:

National Interests: Nations frequently put their own national interests first, which can make collaboration difficult.

Political Differences: Conflicting political beliefs and ideals can make collaboration difficult.

Economic Inequality: Power and influence imbalances can result from economic differences between nations.

Cultural Differences: Misunderstandings and poor communication can occasionally result from cultural differences.

Global Crises: International cooperation may be strained by global crises like pandemics and climate change.

Techniques for Strengthening Global Collaboration

Several tactics can be used to get past these obstacles and improve global cooperation:

Diplomatic Engagement: Resolving disputes and fostering international trust depend on diplomatic discussion and negotiation.

Multilateralism: When it comes to tackling global issues, multilateral cooperation—which involves several nations—can be more successful than bilateral cooperation.

International Institutions: Enforcing international law and coordinating global efforts can both be facilitated by strengthening international institutions.

Public diplomacy: This tactic can promote mutual respect and understanding between countries.

Involving civil society organizations can aid in influencing public opinion and promoting particular policies.

Technology and Innovation: By enabling remote communication and collaboration, technology can promote global cooperation.

Together, nations can overcome obstacles, advance prosperity and peace, and create a brighter future for everybody.

14.3 A Peaceful and Understanding Culture

Building peaceful and sustainable societies requires a culture of understanding and peace. It entails promoting empathy, tolerance, and respect for differences in addition to peacefully and constructively resolving conflict.

The Value of Understanding and Peace

For a number of reasons, a culture of harmony and understanding is essential.

Social Harmony: It lessens social tensions and disputes while fostering social cohesiveness.

Economic Prosperity: Development and expansion of the economy depend on peace and stability.

Environmental Sustainability: The world is better able to handle the world's environmental problems when there is peace and cooperation.

Human Rights: Upholding and advancing human rights requires a culture of harmony and understanding.

Creating a Culture of Understanding and Peace
It takes a multifaceted approach to create a culture of peace and understanding.

Here are a few crucial tactics:

Peace Education:

Including lessons on conflict resolution, empathy, and tolerance in school curricula is known as peace education.
Human Rights Education: Encouraging human rights education to promote dignity and respect for diversity.
Encouraging students to become knowledgeable and involved global citizens is known as global citizenship education.

Intercultural Communication and Dialogue

Cultural Exchange Programs: Encouraging cultural exchange initiatives to foster mutual respect and understanding.
Promoting communication between individuals of various faiths in order to promote tolerance

and understanding is known as interfaith dialogue.

Promoting multicultural education in order to dispel stereotypes and celebrate diversity.

Mediation and Conflict Resolution:

Teaching people how to resolve conflicts and negotiate effectively is known as mediation and negotiation.

In order to address the underlying causes of conflict, peacebuilding initiatives should be supported.

Reconciliation and Dialogue: Promoting communication and reconciliation between parties in conflict.

Critical thinking and media literacy:

Teaching people to evaluate media messages critically and spot bias and false information is known as media literacy.

Developing critical thinking abilities is necessary to assess data and reach well-informed conclusions.

Equity and Social Justice:

In order to ease tensions and foster social harmony, it is important to address both social and economic disparities.

Promoting Human Rights: Ensuring that everyone has the chance to realize their full potential while also defending human rights.

Opportunities and Difficulties

It's a constant struggle to create a culture of harmony and understanding.

Among the main difficulties are:

Violence and Conflict: These two issues have the potential to sabotage efforts to create a culture of peace and disturb social harmony.

Extremism and Intolerance: Attempts to advance understanding and peace may be hampered by extremism and intolerance.

Misinformation and Disinformation: These two types of information have the power to sow division and hatred.

There are plenty of chances to create a world that is more understanding and peaceful in spite of these obstacles. Together, people, groups, and countries can build a future characterized by justice, peace, and respect for human rights.

Individuals' Role

People can make a significant contribution to creating a culture of harmony and understanding by:

Empathy practice involves making an effort to comprehend other people's viewpoints.

Encouraging Tolerance and Respect: Honoring people's differences and combating prejudice.

Talking: Having productive conversations with individuals from various backgrounds.

Endorsing Peace Initiatives: Endorsing groups that advance human rights and peace.

Teaching Others: Teaching others the value of understanding and peace.

Future generations can live in a more peaceful and sustainable world if we adopt a culture of understanding and peace.

Chapter 15:

Conclusion: Embracing Change and Shaping the Future

The world is constantly changing due to societal changes, globalization, and technological breakthroughs. In order to effectively manage these changes, we need to adopt flexibility, creativity, and an optimistic outlook. We can improve the world for present and future generations by accepting change and influencing the course of events.

The Unavoidable Nature of Change

Life will inevitably involve change. It affects our individual experiences as well as the environment we live in, happening on both an individual and societal level. Although change can be unsettling, it also offers chances for advancement, growth, and development. We can put ourselves in a position to seize new opportunities and conquer obstacles by embracing change.

The Strength of Flexibility

The ability to adapt is essential in the quickly evolving world of today. It enables us to flourish in dynamic settings, negotiate uncertainty, and change course in response to fresh information. We can become more resilient and successful by improving our ability to adapt.

Innovation's Significance

Innovation is what propels advancement. It entails developing novel concepts, goods, and procedures that have the potential to enhance our quality of life. We must promote creativity, risk-taking, and an openness to trying new things in order to promote innovation. We can solve difficult issues, develop new sectors of the economy, and raise everyone's standard of living by embracing innovation.

The Function of Technology

Technology has the ability to change industries and societies. Global issues like poverty, illness, and climate change can be addressed with it. But it's crucial to use technology sensibly and morally. We can build a more sustainable and just future by utilizing technology to its full potential.

The Strength of Human Relationships

Human connection is still crucial, even with technology's growing influence. Collaboration, empathy, and the development of solid relationships are essential for both individual and societal well-being. We can make the world kinder and more welcoming by fostering our relationships.

The Value of Moral Leadership

To successfully navigate the challenges of the twenty-first century, ethical leadership is crucial. Leaders who put sustainability, justice, and integrity first can encourage and inspire others to make a difference. We can guarantee that technological innovations are applied for the greater good by encouraging moral conduct and cultivating a culture of accountability.

It is crucial that we prioritize human values, welcome change, and embrace innovation as we navigate the opportunities and challenges of the future. We can build a more equitable, just, and sustainable world if we band together. We have the power to influence the future, and by accepting change and acting, we can create a better world for present and future generations.

15.1 Important Issues and Themes in the Contemporary World

There are many interrelated global opportunities and challenges in the twenty-first century. A number of important themes that will influence humanity's future come to light as we traverse this quickly shifting terrain.

Sustainability of the Environment and Climate Change

Perhaps the most important worldwide issue of our day is climate change. Systems, economies, and societies are at risk due to rising sea levels, extreme weather, and global warming. Reducing greenhouse gas emissions, switching to renewable energy sources, and implementing sustainable practices are all necessary to combat climate change.

Developments in Technology and Digital Transformation

Technological developments are changing economies, societies, and industries. Automation, machine learning, and artificial intelligence are changing the workplace and opening up new possibilities. But these developments also bring up moral questions about security, privacy, and the possibility of job displacement.

Pandemics and World Health

The world's interconnectedness and the vulnerability of global health systems were brought to light by the COVID-19 pandemic. Rapid scientific advancements, a strong healthcare infrastructure, and international cooperation will be necessary to combat future pandemics and health crises.

Social Justice and Economic Inequality

The gap between the rich and the poor is growing, making economic inequality a serious problem. In many regions of the world, social justice problems like poverty, gender inequality, and racial discrimination still exist. A diversified strategy that incorporates social programs, economic policies, and cultural transformation is needed to address these issues.

Global Governance and Political Polarization

The global governance system has been put to the test, and international cooperation has been undermined by political polarization and the rise of nationalism. Addressing global issues like pandemics and climate change requires effective global governance.

Principal Difficulties

Notwithstanding these advantages, the twenty-first century has a number of important obstacles to overcome:

Climate Change: The environment and human society are seriously threatened by the effects of climate change, which include rising sea levels, extreme weather, and biodiversity loss.

Economic Inequality: Increasing economic disparity can result in decreased social mobility, political instability, and social unrest.

Technological Disruption: Economic disruption and job displacement may result from rapid technological change.

Geopolitical Tensions: Geopolitical conflicts and tensions have the potential to erode international security and collaboration.

Global Health Crises: When old diseases resurface and new ones emerge, the results can be disastrous.

In order to overcome these obstacles and create a sustainable future, we need to:

Encourage International Cooperation: Encourage international cooperation to tackle issues such as poverty, inequality, and climate change.

Invest in Research and Education: To create creative answers to global issues, invest in research and education.

Adopt Sustainable Practices: Encourage environmentally friendly methods of energy use, industry, and agriculture.

__Handle Social Inequality:__ Put laws into place that will lessen inequality and advance social justice.

__Strengthen Governance:__ To increase legitimacy and trust, strengthen governance and guarantee accountability.

Together, we can build a brighter future for everybody.

15.2 An Urgent Appeal: Creating a Better Future

It is crucial to acknowledge our shared responsibility for creating a better future as we negotiate the challenges of the twenty-first century. This calls for initiative, a dedication to constructive change, and the readiness to act.

Personal Accountability

Every person has the ability to change things. Making thoughtful decisions and embracing sustainable practices can help create a more just and sustainable world.

Among the doable actions are:

Reduce, Reuse, Recycle: Cut down on waste by recycling materials, reusing products, and reducing consumption.

Conserve Water and Energy: To lessen your impact on the environment, practice water and energy conservation.

Encourage Sustainable Businesses: Select goods and services from businesses that place a high value on ethics and sustainability.

Donate and Volunteer: Contribute to causes that share your values or offer your time to neighborhood organizations.

Educate Both Yourself and Others: Keep up with world events and impart your knowledge to others.

Group Initiatives and Community Involvement

In order to address both local and global issues, community engagement is essential. Communities can bring about constructive change and forge a brighter future by banding together.

Here are a few strategies for interacting with your community:

Engage in Local Government: Contact elected officials, attend town hall meetings, and cast your ballot in elections.

Join Community Groups: Take part in neighborhood groups and donate your time to assist others.

Support Local Businesses: To help small businesses and the local economy, shop locally.

Plan Community Events: Plan charitable events, food drives, and clean-up days, among other community activities.

Encourage Change: Encourage laws that advance environmental preservation, social justice, and sustainability.

International Collaboration

Global problems demand global answers. Addressing problems like poverty, inequality, and climate change requires international cooperation.

People can support international initiatives by:

Giving to or volunteering for international organizations that tackle global issues is one way to support them.

Promoting Fair Trade: To guarantee that workers in developing nations receive fair compensation, support fair trade initiatives.

Reducing Your Carbon Footprint: Use sustainable modes of transportation and cut back on your use of fossil fuels to lessen your carbon footprint.

Educating Others: Spread knowledge about world problems and motivate people to act.

Accepting the Future of Sustainability

The transition to a more just, fair, and ecologically sustainable world is necessary for a sustainable future. We can build a better future for ourselves and future generations by adopting sustainable practices, fighting for social justice, and cooperating to solve global issues. We all have a responsibility to act and change things.

Keep in mind that every little step matters. We can all work together to make the world more sustainable, just, and peaceful by choosing wisely and acting.

15.3 A Positive Outlook on the Future

It's easy to feel overpowered by the difficulties that lie ahead as we negotiate the complexity of the twenty-first century. Nevertheless, there is a great chance for a better future despite the uncertainty. a future in which human ingenuity, innovation, and technology come together to build a more sustainable, just, and equitable world.

A World of Plenty and Parity

One of the most optimistic future scenarios is one in which technology is employed to solve global issues. Biotechnology, machine learning, and artificial intelligence have the potential to completely transform energy production, healthcare, and agriculture. We can imagine a time when there is no more hunger, no more diseases, and plenty of clean energy thanks to advancements in these areas.

Furthermore, we can work toward a society in which everyone has access to basic essentials like food, water, and shelter and economic inequality is lessened. We can strive toward a more equitable future by supporting fair trade policies, making investments in healthcare and education, and empowering underserved communities.

A Planet That Is Sustainable

An optimistic future also requires environmental sustainability. We can preserve our planet for coming generations by switching to renewable energy sources, cutting back on our carbon footprint, and implementing sustainable practices.

Renewable Energy: We can lessen our dependency on fossil fuels and slow down climate change by utilizing the energy of the sun, wind, and water.

Circular Economy: We can lessen our impact on the environment, conserve resources, and minimize waste by implementing a circular economy model.

Sustainable Agriculture: Using sustainable agricultural methods can help safeguard the environment and guarantee food security.

A Peaceful World Community

Human progress requires a future marked by harmony, collaboration, and understanding. By encouraging intercultural communication, advancing diplomacy, and peacefully settling disputes, we can create a more peaceful world community.

Cultural Exchange: Promoting tolerance and fostering cross-cultural communication can help heal divisions.
Working together with other countries to address global issues like poverty and climate change is known as international cooperation.
Human Rights and Social Justice: A world that is equitable and peaceful depends on upholding human rights and advancing social justice.

Individuals' Role

Individuals are vital in determining the future, even though global issues necessitate group efforts. We can help create a more sustainable and equitable world by making thoughtful decisions like cutting back on consumption, volunteering, and supporting change.

We cannot predict the future. We have the power to mold it. We can build a prosperous and just world by embracing innovation, encouraging sustainability, and cultivating collaboration. The rewards are incalculable, but the journey may be difficult.

www.ingramcontent.com/pod-product-compliance
Lightning Source LLC
Chambersburg PA
CBHW061622250726

48659CB00004B/1042